Hayne, Coe
    Baptist trail-makers of Michigan.
Berrien Springs,Mich., Hardscrabble Books/
Judson Press, (1977c.1936.)
    180p.   illus.

    1.Baptist Church - Michigan - History.
2.Michigan - Pioneer life. 3.Michigan -
History.   I.Title.

BAPTIST TRAIL-MAKERS
OF MICHIGAN

1977

A Hardscrabble Reprint

*Reprinted with the cooperation of
The Judson Press*

ISBN- 0-915056-06-2

Printed in the United States of America

**HARDSCRABBLE BOOKS
BERRIEN SPRINGS, MICHIGAN**

LEWIS CASS

Civil Governor of Michigan, 1813-1831

BAPTIST TRAIL-MAKERS
OF MICHIGAN

By COE HAYNE

Author of

*Red Men On the Bighorn, Vanguard of the Caravans,
They Came Seeking, etc.*

———

Published for

THE CENTENNIAL COMMITTEE

OF

THE MICHIGAN BAPTIST STATE CONVENTION

1836   **1936**

BY

THE JUDSON PRESS

PHILADELPHIA

| BOSTON | CHICAGO | LOS ANGELES |
| KANSAS CITY | SEATTLE | TORONTO |

PRINTED IN U. S. A.

CONTENTS

Contents

FOREWORD AND DEDICATION

This book is presented to the Baptists of Michigan in response to the request of the Centennial Committee of the Michigan Baptist State Convention. Its production has been made possible by the cooperative action of the Michigan Baptist State Convention, The American Baptist Publication Society, the Department of Missionary Education of the Board of Education of the Northern Baptist Convention, and The American Baptist Home Mission Society.

The making of the book has been a source of joy. Treasured memories have been stirred. . . A native of Michigan, whose father was pastor of Michigan churches during thirty-eight years, the writer dedicates the volume to Michigan Baptist folks, old and young, who now must be the " Pioneers of the New Century."

As in imagination we follow the paths carved out of the wilderness by our pioneering fathers, may our trust in the Christ they served be strengthened and our love for the wonderful Commonwealth they helped to found be renewed.

❋❋❋

For materials and helpful guidance the writer gratefully acknowledges his indebtedness to Ralph Taylor Andem, H. C. Gleiss, Albert H. Finn, George H. Waid, Albert L. Scott, William Ashmore, Jr., Ernest E. Rogers, H. H. Savage, Mrs. William H.

Foreword and Dedication

Dorrance, Charles True Goodsell, Mrs. George Wreggit, Mrs. Leslie E. Swain, Miss Florence E. Grant, John E. Smith, Thomas T. Leete, Jr., Mrs. Kathleen Penrose, Miss Jessie K. Bates, J. W. Mauck, Willfred Mauck, Lorenzo Dow, Willis F. Dunbar, Miss Helen E. Slayton, Mrs. Della Reynolds McIntyre, Miss Harrietta L. Reynolds, the Public Libraries of New York City and Hillsdale, Kalamazoo Public Library and Museum, *The Missionary Review of the World, Missions,* Harper and Brothers, Publishers, the Woman's American Baptist Foreign Mission Society, the American Baptist Foreign Mission Society, the Woman's American Baptist Home Mission Society, and the Michigan Pioneer and Historical Society.

DECEMBER 7, 1935.   C. H.

LIST OF ILLUSTRATIONS

I

AWAKENING OF BAPTISTS IN THE UNITED STATES

While the historic background of the world-wide Baptist communion is rooted in the origins of Christianity, two movements in the history of the Protestant churches gave particular impetus to the early growth and solidarity of Baptists in America: (1) The Great Awakening that began in New England in 1740; (2) The Missionary Movement that began when the Baptist Missionary Society was organized, October 2, 1792, at Kettering, England, in the church of Andrew Fuller as the result of a memorable sermon preached by William Carey at a meeting of his Association held at Nottingham, May 30, 1792. The two divisions of that famous discourse were: "Expect great things from God; attempt great things for God."

During the first century after the Baptists began their operations in the United States, that is up to the year 1750, there were only about fifty-eight churches which acquired any durability.[1] Rhode Island led with sixteen churches; then New Jersey with ten; Massachusetts, nine; Connecticut, nine; Pennsylvania, seven; South Carolina, three; New York, two; Delaware, one; Maine, one.

[1] Benedict, *History of the Baptists*, p. 365.

Baptist Trail-Makers in Michigan

THE GREAT AWAKENING

In September, 1740, George Whitefield of England began his preaching in Boston. The spiritual awakening under this evangelist and others, including Jonathan Edwards, the Tennents and the Wesleys, was opposed with great vehemence, but there resulted a powerful revival, ". . . such as New England had never seen. A torpid community was aroused as by the trump of God, from its long and heavy slumber; ministers and people were converted; the style of preaching and the tone of individual piety were improved; a cold, cadaverous formalism gave place to the living energy of experimental godliness; the doctrines of the gospel were brought out from their concealment, and made to reassert their claims to a cordial, practical credence, and all the interests of truth and holiness received new homage from regenerated thousands." [2]

At the commencement of the great revival the Baptists of New England were slow in taking an active part therein; yet there was no denomination that reaped a more bountiful harvest therefrom. The Separatist and New Light movements had direct bearing upon the growth and character of our churches.

Not in Massachusetts alone did the Baptist cause profit by the Great Awakening, nor in New England alone; throughout both North and South Baptists were greatly augmented in numbers under the stimulus of evangelistic preaching.

[2] Benedict, *History of the Baptists*, p. 392.

THE MISSIONARY MOVEMENT

The missionary movement that began with Carey welded Baptists in the United States as well as in England into a body spiritually militant and purposeful. Its benign influence was felt in all Christian communions.

When Samuel J. Mills, son of a scholarly Congregational minister in Torringford, Connecticut, in April, 1806, entered Williams College, he began at once to exert a decided religious influence upon the student body. His diary covering this period contains many fervent expressions of a desire to acquire the spirit of prayer. A praying group was formed that afforded Mills, now twenty-three years of age, special opportunities to give voice to his religious enthusiasms. On Wednesdays the members of this praying band were accustomed to meet under the willows south of what was known as West College, and on Saturdays at a greater distance from the campus, half-way to the Hoosac River, in a maple grove called Sloan's Meadow.

On a hot August day three freshmen and two sophomores of Williams College were in conference in a grove when a thunder-storm compelled them to seek shelter beneath a haystack near-by. The freshmen were Samuel J. Mills, James Richards, and Harvey Loomis; the sophomores, Francis L. Robbins and Byram Green. As these young men went into that enforced huddle, their conversation shifted to Asia. Mills' earnestness was communicated to the others. He proposed sending the gospel to dispel the darkness in that land. "We can do it if we will," he declared. His great faith in prayer impelled him to challenge his companions to step out with him into a world of larger horizons.

"Come," pleaded Mills, "let us make it a subject of prayer under this haystack, while the dark clouds are going and the clear sky is coming."

One by one they prayed.

The site of the sheltering haystack that had been a temple divinely blessed, is now marked by an appropriate monument, bearing the inscription, "The Birthplace of American Foreign Missions."

The meetings in the grove were continued until cold weather, when an observant woman on the road offered her kitchen for the purpose. The names of five students have been mentioned. In addition to them the following were members of the group: John Nelson, Calvin Bushnell, Rufus Pomeroy, Samuel Ware, Edwin Dwight, and Ezra Fisk. Later Luther Rice and Gordon Hall joined the band. Before these young men left Williams they had given expression to their missionary zeal in the form of an organization called a "Society of Brethren," the first foreign missionary society in America. In a room on the ground floor of old East College they resolved, secretly, to project a society that should have for its object "to effect in the persons of its members a mission, or missions to the heathen." They were to become pioneers, explorers. None of their countrymen had gone before them. They did not ask anybody outside of their ranks to go on a mission they were unwilling to undertake. The first

ADONIRAM JUDSON

signers of the constitution of the "Brethren" were Samuel J. Mills, Ezra Fisk, James Richards, John Seward, and Luther Rice. They sought to enlist the interest and cooperation of such eminent ministers as Doctors Worcester, Griffin, Morse, and Dana. These men gave them friendly and helpful advice. After graduation the young men scattered to other colleges to start similar societies but to meet with indifferent success; later six of them came together at Andover for theological training, bringing glowing embers to kindle a world-conflagration.

"That such a movement should have originated with the undergraduates of a college, at a time," said Mark Hopkins, "when there was so much in the state of the world to excite the youthful imagination and fire ambition and distract the mind, when Europe was quaking under the tread of the man of destiny, and the country was fearfully excited by political divisions, can only be accounted for from the special agency of the Spirit of God."

When the scene of the activities of the Brethren shifted from Williams College to Andover Seminary, in 1809, they became associated with several other students of similar sentiments, among whom were Samuel Nott, Jr., of Union College, Adoniram Judson, of Brown, and Samuel Newell, of Harvard. Gordon Hall, of Williams, in time also joined the Andover group. The Brethren brought from Williams their constitution.

Adoniram Judson could not be enrolled as a regular student at Andover upon entrance in 1808, as he was not a professed Christian. A gradual change came over him within the year and the hope of entering the ministry became his without an attending doubt. In 1809, he read Claudius Buchanan's *Star in the East,* which gave him a vivid conception of his duty to the destitute peoples of foreign lands. The tremendous change that came over him at this time is best described by Judson in a letter to Luther Rice written years afterward:

"MY DEAR BROTHER RICE:

" You ask me to give you some account of my first missionary impressions, and those of my earliest associates. Mine were occasioned by reading Buchanan's *Star in the East,* in the year 1809, at the Andover Theological Seminary. . . For some days I was unable to attend to the studies of my class, and spent my time in wondering at my past stupidity, depicting the most romantic scenes in missionary life, and roving about the college rooms, declaiming on the subject of missions. My views were very incorrect, and my feelings extravagant; but yet I have always felt thankful to God for bringing me into that state of excitement, which was perhaps necessary, in the first instance, to enable me to break the strong attachment I felt to home and country, and to endure the thought of abandoning all my wonted pursuits and animating prospects. That excitement soon passed away; but it left a strong desire to prosecute my inquiries, and ascertain the path of duty."

Alone in the woods back of the college, after a period of quiet meditation and prayer, Judson surrendered to his conviction that his life should be devoted to efforts in behalf of the destitute in foreign lands. Nott, his classmate, was considering the subject, but had not arrived at a definite decision. It was at this critical juncture that Mills, Richards, and others came to Andover from Williams. In the summer of 1810, a petition signed by Judson, Nott, Mills, and Newell was presented to the General (Congregational) Association of Massachusetts, meeting in Bradford, in which they solicited the "advice, direction, and prayers" of their "fathers in the church" in relation to the following inquiries: "Whether, with their present views and feelings, they ought to renounce the object of missions, as either visionary or impracticable; if not, whether they ought to direct their attention to the Eastern or the Western world; whether they may expect patronage and support from a missionary society in this country, or must commit themselves to the direction of a European society; and what preparatory measures they ought to take previous to actual engagement."

This modest yet stirring petition led to the immediate formation of the American Board of Commissioners for Foreign Missions "for the purpose of devising ways and means, and adopting and prosecuting measures, for promoting the spread of the gospel in heathen lands." The Commissioners voted to commend the young petitioners to the grace of God and advised them "to humbly wait the openings

and guidance of Providence in respect to their great
and excellent design," and, in the meantime, to give
"diligent attention to suitable studies and means
of information."

Two years later a notable service was held in the
Tabernacle Congregational Church at Salem, Massachusetts, when Adoniram Judson, Gordon Hall, Samuel Nott, Jr., Samuel Newell, and Luther Rice, were
ordained to the ministry. Near Judson knelt his
beautiful young bride, Ann Hasseltine Judson. Their
marriage had occurred the day before. Ann's friend,
Miss Harriet Atwood, who three days later became
the wife of Samuel Newell, was in the audience, an
interested listener if not an actual participant in
the ceremony. The ordination occurred February 2,
1812, and before the end of the month the seven
missionaries had sailed for India, the Judsons and
the Newells, on the *Caravan,* and Nott, Hall, and
Rice on the *Harmony.*

During the long voyage around the Cape of Good
Hope to Calcutta, Judson spent many hours in a
study of the subject of baptism as viewed by Baptists in preparation of a possible discussion of the
subject with the noted English missionary, William
Carey. He may have been surprised, however,
when, upon landing, the mention of Baptist views
was omitted by Carey and his associates, Marshman
and Ward, not an uncommon courtesy among Baptists. Judson did not at once reveal the change
that had taken place in his thinking. In his change
of sentiments he was not alone. Both Adoniram
and Ann Judson were baptized at Calcutta on Sep-

tember 6, 1812. Consequently they faced the painful necessity of discontinuing their connection with the American Board of Commissioners. In his letter to Dr. S. M. Worcester, corresponding secretary of the Congregational body, he revealed his distress:

" The dissolution of my connection with the Board of Commissioners, and a separation from my dear missionary brethren, I consider (the) most distressing consequences of my late change of sentiments, and indeed, the most distressing events which have ever befallen me. I have now the prospect before me of going alone to some distant island, unconnected with any society at present existing, from which I might be furnished with assistant laborers or pecuniary support. Whether the Baptist churches in America will compassionate my situation, I know not. I hope, therefore, that while my friends condemn what they deem a departure from the truth, they will at least pity me and pray for me."

To the Baptists of America, through letters addressed to Thomas Baldwin and Lucius Bolles, came the offer from Judson to serve as a missionary under their auspices.

"Alone in this foreign land," wrote Judson to Lucius Bolles, " I make my appeal to those whom, with their permission, I will call my Baptist brethren in the United States." To Thomas Baldwin the following—a call to an entire people, summoning them to world service: " Should there be formed ... a Baptist Society, for the support of a mission in these parts, *I shall be ready to consider myself their missionary.*"

Although compelled for conscience' sake to sever his connection with the American Board of Commissioners, Judson retained a strong affection for that far-seeing band of missionary pioneers. To Dr. Rufus Anderson, corresponding secretary of the Congregational Board, in 1839, he wrote: " Though I have been (as some may think) a wayward son of the American Board of Commissioners for Foreign Missions, I have always retained the warmest filial affection for that body, under whose auspices I first came out."

Shortly after the baptism of Adoniram and Ann Judson, Luther Rice became convinced that he should take the same radical step.

After many difficulties and hardships, many of them being intensified if not caused by the state of war existing between Great Britain and the United States, the Judsons made their way by devious routes to Rangoon, Burma, the scene of their life-long missionary labors that resulted in the foundation of one of the largest Protestant mission fields in the world.

In the meantime Luther Rice returned to the United States with the full approval of the Judsons to lead in a movement that had for its aim the awakening of men and women everywhere, in remote localities as well as in populous cities, to accept a God-given share in a mighty task in behalf of the unevangelized peoples of the world that the courage and convictions of Adoniram and Ann Judson and Luther Rice suddenly had brought to their doors. Equally indebted are Baptists as well as other evan-

From Engraving published in "Ladies Repository," 1860

ANN HASSELTINE JUDSON

gelical communions to Samuel J. Mills, Samuel Newell, and other members of that first group of Brethren who blazed trails and set lights for others to follow.

II

THE GOSPEL PIONEER OF THE WEST [1]

A never-to-be-forgotten event in the life of John Mason Peck, the young pastor of a small Baptist flock in Amenia, New York, occurred in June, 1815, when he met Luther Rice at an Associational meeting and heard him speak. Rice had just returned from Burma to conduct one of the most impressive series of public appeals that church history records. The name of Adoniram Judson, his companion in a great adventure, was spoken frequently by this ardent young spirit who had been commissioned by the Baptist Board of Foreign Missions to post from one State to another to arouse the churches to a sense of their unprecedented opportunity in foreign mission fields. Luther Rice was a flaming torch. His stirring message, in which he portrayed the destitution and degradation of millions of people who had never heard the gospel, set the soul of John Mason Peck on fire. The two young men discovered that they had much in common although Luther Rice was well educated while the other was merely a lonely searcher who had advanced but a little way in the several branches of an English education. The pastor from Amenia persuaded his new-found friend to go home with him. The story John heard

[1] Adapted from *Vanguard of the Caravans,* by Coe Hayne. The Judson Press, 1931.

from Luther Rice forms a golden chapter in the history of world missions.

The night John and Sally Peck entertained Luther Rice in the Baptist parsonage at Amenia proved to be a turning-point in their lives. Before their guest departed, a plan was concocted whereby John was to obtain a leave of absence from his church and go out as Luther Rice's agent to visit two or three Associations in Central New York to promote interest in missions. The commission engaged the young man's heart and mind to the full and served to fan to glowing heat the desire to identify himself with the work that Luther Rice had described so graphically. The record of his first itinerary in behalf of foreign missions shows that he rode four hundred and forty miles, delivered nineteen addresses, and took five missionary collections.

" How greatly favored I am! . . I share and rejoice in the light of life," recorded John Mason Peck, September 14, 1815.

On the first day of May, in 1816, John Mason Peck was on his way to Philadelphia to begin a year's study in the home of William Staughton, corresponding secretary of the Baptist Board of Foreign Missions in the United States and pastor of the Sansom Street Baptist Church in Philadelphia. Sally and her little ones, now three in number, were left at Amenia.

On May 15, 1817, Peck applied to the Baptist Board of Foreign Missions for appointment as a missionary on the Western Frontier.

" Six o'clock," recorded Peck on May 19, 1817.

" The long agony is over. The Board have accepted Mr. Welch and myself as missionaries to the Missouri Territory during our and their pleasure; and have appropriated the sum of one thousand dollars to defray our expenses in getting to St. Louis and for the support of the mission. . . I have put my hand to the plow. O Lord, may I never turn back—never regret this step. It is my desire to live, to labor, to die as a kind of pioneer in advancing the gospel."

Thus did Peck's generous spirit respond to the needs of the struggling American frontier communities.

The years to follow held answers to his threefold prayer; he became known as the Gospel Pioneer.

A small one-horse wagon belonging to John Mason Peck stood in front of the home of Asa Peck on the afternoon of July 25, 1817, ready for a long overland journey from Litchfield, Connecticut, to St. Louis, Missouri. Within the house Asa and Hannah knelt with their only son, his wife, and their three children. Hannah, strong in faith, spoke the words that gave John the courage to go through with the ordeal of parting: " If the Lord hath need of him— only son as he is, and we are growing old—let his holy will be done! He gave, and though very precious to us was this his gift, yet, if there is a needs be for the sacrifice, God forbid that I should hinder his devotement to his Saviour and mine."

Nine years later John returned to take his mother to the Illinois country. He never saw his father again on earth.

A keel-boat with John Mason Peck and his family

JOHN MASON PECK

aboard arrived at the foot of Elm Street, St. Louis, early in the morning of December 1, 1817.

On the corner of Myrtle and Main Streets Peck succeeded in renting a single room for his family. No other shelter was obtainable in the roaring village which was crowded with a motley, questing aggregation of people. In his restricted quarters Peck lay ill two months with a fever that had prostrated him eleven days before leaving the keel-boat.

St. Louis in 1817, no longer merely a French trading-post, was awakening to a consciousness of its importance as the gateway to the West. Still bearing the marks reminiscent of Spanish and French rule, the village was receiving to itself a restless, property-hungry populace too rapidly to house properly. Many newcomers were transients waiting for the coming of the spring in order to travel elsewhere. Every dwelling-house was crowded. Save Bellissame's French tavern for farmers, there was not a hotel or boarding-house in the place. The merchants for the most part cooked their meals and slept in the small buildings in which they sold their goods. Rentals and food prices were high. A barrel of flour cost twelve dollars, sugar from thirty to forty cents per pound, coffee from sixty-two to seventy-five. Products brought in from the range were not cheap for the times—butter fifty cents per pound, eggs fifty cents per dozen, and pork from six to eight dollars per hundred pounds. Under the necessity of exercising strict economy in all of their expenditures, the Peck family was faced with serious living problems from the outset.

In recalling those trying days, Peck declared that neither the excessive prices for every article of food in St. Louis nor the extreme inconvenience of his living accommodations awakened his concern as much as did the state of religion and morals in St. Louis and neighboring settlements.

Rarely has a missionary faced conditions more adverse to the growth of Christian churches than did John Mason Peck when he arrived in St. Louis.

Half the population of the village was made up of Anglo-Americans who were " infidels of a low and indecent grade. . . This class despised and vilified religion in every form, were vulgarly profane, even to the worst forms of blasphemy, and," added Peck, " poured out scoffings and contempt on the few Christians in the village. Their nightly orgies were scenes of drunkenness and profane revelry. Among the frantic rites observed were the mock celebration of the Lord's Supper and burning the Bible. . . The boast was often made that *the Sabbath never had crossed and never should cross the Mississippi.*"

" St. Louis must not be relinquished by the Baptists," wrote John Mason Peck three years after his arrival at his distant post in his appeal to the Baptist Board of Foreign Missions to reconsider the resolution concerning his removal to the Indian mission station in the Indian Territory. He could not retreat now. His driving passion was to see the banner of the Cross planted firmly in the Mississippi Valley.

Nearly forty years later Peck made the following observation: " There are now (in St. Louis) as great a proportion of pious Christian church-members and of church-going people, in the ratio of the whole population, as in Philadelphia, New York, or any other large commercial city in our country."

In 1823, when Massachusetts Baptists came to the rescue of the Western Mission, Peck had become a real builder, conscious of a plan and a program. The days of hesitations and fear were behind him. A pathfinder who sensed the nakedness and destitution accompanying the birth of an empire, it was given him to remain at his chosen station long enough to enable him to have a large share in " guiding the thoughts, molding the manners, and forming the institutions of the West."

The home John Mason Peck established at Rock Spring, Ill., not over thirty miles from St. Louis, became Baptist headquarters for that vast unevangelized section.

He was a real pioneer. With the knowledge that he had of the great migrations setting westward, he constructed the picture of countless communities in the Mississippi Valley destitute of gospel privileges, destitute even of the rudiments of a decent public school system. He foresaw on the American frontier as great a missionary opportunity as Judson and Rice had seen in the Orient. He became a competent rider of the dim trails of the Western frontier. His travels to the remote settlements in Missouri and Illinois were made in the saddle or on foot. There were practically no roads. The " traces " he followed through the wooded tracts and over the Mississippi River bottoms and barrens were often obliterated by the overflow of the swollen streams; his paths to his appointments were at their best mere bridle-trails. His pallet in the poor squatter homes he visited in most cases was his saddle-blanket laid upon a puncheon floor with his saddle for a pillow. He quickly adapted himself to the hardships of the trail as he brought to the frontier a body inured to toil and privation and a soul fired with the desire to meet life with all of its vicissitudes cheerfully and helpfully.

John Mason Peck created the influences which induced Jonathan Going, of Massachusetts, to make a survey of the Western field and led to the formation of The American Baptist Home Mission Society in 1832. Christian education found no champion in the growing settlements more zealous than this tireless itinerant missionary. He not only became the founder of Shurtleff College in 1827 (then known as the Rock Spring Theological and High School), but in 1842 accepted election as the Corresponding Secretary of The American Baptist Publication Society. He always was an enthusiastic advocate of Sunday schools.

Where the need was greatest during the years that followed, our Pioneer was found waging a patient warfare of faith and courage, of ceaseless toil and of poverty. The activities of the man who became known and loved as the "Sage of Rock Spring," cooperating with his neighbors in behalf of a wilderness empire in ways seldom paralleled, furnished the elements of a story that may never be told in its entirety.

The Gospel Pioneer of the West

Four years after the Home Mission Society was formed as a result of Peck's vision and labors, the Michigan Baptist Convention came into being to cooperate with the Home Mission Society in the establishment of churches in Michigan and other parts of our country, to foster Christian education and to help send the gospel message to foreign lands. The Michigan Convention was organized in Detroit, August 31–September 1, 1836.

III

MICHIGAN'S FIRST BAPTIST CHURCH

When General George Rogers Clark, a Virginian residing in Kentucky, with a hundred and fifty men and two pieces of artillery, after a march quite unparalleled in history, captured Vincennes from the British defenders under Colonel Hamilton, February 25, 1779, he created a situation that caused the boundary between the United States and British America to be the Great Lakes instead of the Ohio River. Michigan, a part of this great Northwest Territory, was left pretty much to the Indians and the traders until 1818 when some of the lands in southern Michigan were surveyed and sold to settlers. Land speculators in the East anxious to sell their holdings in Ohio, Indiana, and Illinois, had helped to spread the rumor that Michigan Territory was a land of impassable swamps and dismal forests, unfit for settlement.

On August 27, 1818, a small steamboat, named the *Walk-in-the-Water*, after an old Wyandotte chief, arrived at Detroit. The whole countryside turned out to gaze upon her and marvel at this miracle in water transportation. Michigan, late in receiving the notice of home-seekers because of the unfavorable reports of the surveyor-general, now came into her own.

DETROIT IN 1820

From Collections in the New York Public Library

On the strength of favorable reports of exploring parties covering a portion of Michigan bordering Clinton River, the Pontiac Company was formed November 5, 1818. This was a business venture sponsored and directed mainly by Detroit people to found a village (Pontiac) and sell land. Col. Stephen Mack was manager and Judge Solomon Sibley was one of the partners. The region was one of great natural beauty, a wilderness of lakes, forests and oak openings, and soon became a center of attraction for oncoming emigrants from New England, New York, and Pennsylvania.

Among the folks back east who had learned that the early unfavorable reports concerning the Territory of Michigan were unfounded was Orisson Allen, of Niagara County, New York. Less than a year after John Mason Peck arrived at St. Louis, this layman with his family started out for the new country with the high hopes of an adventuring pioneer. On the twentieth of October, 1818, they with other passengers boarded a sailing vessel at Buffalo bound for Detroit. Because of strong adverse winds the schooner was driven back three times to Erie, Pennsylvania. Twenty-eight days after leaving Buffalo the craft with her weary passengers put in at L'Anse Cruex. From this point some of the passengers, including the Orisson Allen and Joseph Todd families, journeyed in wagons to Mt. Clemens.

In December, following a heavy snow-storm, Orisson Allen, Joseph Todd and the latter's son (later known as Major J. J. Todd), and a Mr. Thornton, started out on foot to explore the country that is

c   [21]

now Oakland County.[1] Each man carried a supply
of provisions, a blanket, and an ax and two men
packed their rifles. At the end of the first day's
hike camp was made on the site of the future town
of Romeo.

The snow was a foot deep and how to spend the
night comfortably with but one blanket per man
was a problem these hardy pioneers solved ingeni-
ously. They cut down a hollow basswood-tree and
chopped off two logs seven feet long and split them
open. Then each man took a half-log, placed it near
the fire, wrapped his blanket about him, and slept
soundly in his rude cradle. On the following day
the party arrived at the place where the city of Pontiac now is and where they camped that night, possibly in a log house owned by the Pontiac Company.

It is recorded that all were pleased with the location and concluded that Pontiac would be their
future home. Special interest in these first settlers
on the spot now occupied by the city of Pontiac natu-
rally centers about Orisson Allen because of his—
and Mrs. Allen's—association with those who organized the first Baptist Church in Michigan.

On January 14, 1819, Orisson Allen and family
with Messrs. Todd, Allen, and Thornton and their
families, left Mt. Clemens with Pontiac as their
destination. They traveled in two wagons drawn by
oxen, occasionally being obliged to cut their way
through the tangled undergrowth in forest and

[1] On March 28, 1820, the Governor of Michigan issued a proclama-
tion organizing the County of Oakland and fixing the seat of justice
at Pontiac.

Michigan's First Baptist Church

swamp. They arrived at Pontiac, January 16, 1819.[2]
There was but one log house in the place and this
was owned by the Pontiac Company. It had no bed
chamber, no chimney, no floor except some split logs
upon which beds could be laid. But here lived the
four families,[3] numbering at least fourteen persons
in all, until April. And they were in desperate circumstances. Every bit of food except wild game
and fish had to be brought in from Detroit over a
road that was so bad that a team at times had all it
could do to draw half a load. Before the ground
broke up that spring, Orisson Allen bought a barrel
of flour in Detroit and hired some one to haul it to
Birmingham. From Birmingham to Pontiac, Allen
carried the flour on his back as needed, thirty or
forty pounds to the trip. By June nearly all food
supplies were exhausted together with what little
money Orisson Allen had in his possession when he
arrived at Pontiac. In his extremity he went to
Detroit to interview Judge Sibley with the hope that
this resourceful member of the Pontiac Company
might find a way to help him out of his difficulties.
Orisson Allen later related what took place when
he entered the judge's office and told him that he
must leave Pontiac.[4]

[2] In an account read by Mrs. E. M. Sheldon Stewart at the annual
meeting of the Michigan State Pioneer Society, June 14, 1883, February (1819), instead of January, is given as the month in which the
Todd, Lester, and Allen families arrived at Pontiac.

[3] In the Stewart paper (*Michigan Historical Collections*, Vol. 6, pp.
384, 385), Orisson Allen is reported to have mentioned but three
families in this party, omitting that of Mr. Thornton. Mr. Thornton
is included in the "Reminiscence" of Major J. J. Todd, page 86,
History of Oakland County, by Samuel W. Durant.

[4] *Michigan Historical Collections*, Vol. 6, pp. 384, 385. Used by
permission.

" He asked the reason," said Allen, " and I told him if I stayed there I should starve; my money was gone, and there was no work to be had; it was the only time I had ever known want. The judge buried his face in his hands and sat silent for some time. Finally he said:

" 'You must not leave; we will furnish you with food and you may pay when you can.'

" I said no; I might not be able to pay, and then I should wrong him.

" ' We need more help,' said the judge, ' and if you will stay we will give you employment and I will direct our agent to furnish you with provisions.'

" Early in the spring of 1819 the Pontiac Company had built a large trading-house 20 x 60 feet, and divided into three rooms, and stocked with goods for the Indian trade and provisions for the men in their employ. It was from this agency that Judge Sibley promised me supplies.

" The next morning after this interview I started for Pontiac with a number of men employed by the company, three oxen and a cart, and one woman as passenger. We had to cross a swamp about six miles wide, which was like a sea of mud; the team got stuck and the woman was obliged to wade out.

" I reached home at dark and my wife brought me a piece of bread about half as large as my hand, all the food there was in the house. I could not eat it, nor could I rest that night from fatigue and anxiety.

" Early the next morning I went to the trading-house to learn the judge's orders, and was rejoiced to find that they were, ' Let Mr. Allen have all the provisions he wants.'

" Pork, flour, beans, a very few potatoes and tea was the entire list of supplies, but I was glad enough for a share of these."

Orisson Allen, Joseph Todd, William Lester, and Mr. Thornton in the spring of 1819 worked cooperatively in the erection of a log house for each family. When this job was completed they went to work for the Pontiac Company cutting, hewing and hauling timber for a grist-mill and a saw-mill, both to be run by water-power obtained from Clinton River.

In June, 1822, Mr. and Mrs. Abner Davis settled on their farm one mile east of the court-house. A few weeks later the news was circulated that a meeting would be held at the Gibb's home two miles from the Abner Davis place for the purpose of forming into a church the few Baptists who had settled in Pontiac and vicinity. Mrs. Davis told her husband that she would like to attend this gathering and Abner, although not at the time particularly interested in religion, was quite willing to accompany his wife. At least he told her that it was a long walk and that he would not allow her to undertake it alone. In a letter to the First Baptist Church of Pontiac, written fifty years later, Mrs. Davis recounted the experiences of that night.

" The first obstacle we met was the Clinton River, there being no bridge. A tree had fallen from a high bank, slanting down across the river. I said I would go back, but he said no, he would help me across.

He broke a long stick for a cane, which I took in my right hand, he taking hold of my left, and succeeded in reaching the other end in safety. The first mile there had been a wagon through—the second there was nothing but blazed trees to guide our steps. The meeting was held in Deacon Gibbs' house, which was a frame building with one room. The outside was covered with wide, rough oak boards, and there was a loose floor, with no fireplace, the cooking being done by the side of a log in the dooryard. In this house the Baptist church was organized."

David Douglas opened the meeting and read some "Articles of Faith and Covenant." Those who that night assented to them and requested that their names be recorded as constituent members of the church were Orisson Allen and wife, Mrs. Lemuel Castle, Miss Drusilla Castle, Judah Church, Mrs. Abner Davis, David Douglas and wife, Deacon Gibbs and wife, Mrs. Enoch Hotchkiss, Joseph Lee and wife, Amos Niles, Mrs. William Philips, and Dr. Ziba Swan and wife. Their names are recorded here because they were the Baptist pioneers in the wilderness between the Great Lakes and formed the first church of that communion in the then territory of Michigan.

In the fall of the same year (1822) there came to Michigan Rev. Elon Galusha, sent to the territory by the New York Baptist State Convention. He was at the time pastor of the Baptist Church in Whitesborough, New York. During his missionary tour he visited Pontiac and conducted a service in which the newly formed church was recognized. The little house of Deacon Gibbs was filled with people who came to witness the simple ceremony and hear this gifted man of God preach.

Michigan has been fortunate in the character of the founders of its institutions. Elon Galusha was of a distinguished family. Son of Governor Galusha, of Vermont, he began his ministry early in life. It is related of him that few men could sway a congregation more powerfully than could Mr. Galusha when his sympathies were enlisted. For many years he was one of the best-known ministers in the State of New York, serving the churches for a term as president of the New York Missionary Convention. In addition to the one in Whitesborough he held pastorates at Utica, Rochester, Perry, and Lockport. He was the second ordained Baptist minister to visit Michigan of whom we have record. Isaac McCoy in February, 1821, had visited Governor Cass in Detroit to consult him concerning help for the Indian Mission at Fort Wayne, Indiana.[5] In 1822 McCoy entered the Michigan territory as a missionary to the Potawatomi Indians.

The first ordained minister to settle and labor in Pontiac was Elkanah Comstock. He came in 1824. Michigan Baptists do well to honor his memory as "Michigan's first Baptist pastor," keeping in mind, of course, that Isaac McCoy had begun work among the Indians at the Carey Mission (Niles) two years before Comstock entered the State.

As we contemplate the labors of Elkanah Com-

---

[5] *History of Baptist Indian Missions,* by Isaac McCoy. Washington, D. C., 1840.

stock in Michigan and the contribution members of
his family have made to that Commonwealth we
are led to record that the Wolverine State once
more was blessed in the person of one of her " back-
bone pioneers." This able pathfinder came from
the New England family of Comstocks that helped
to build the foundations of New London, Connecticut. Born in New London, September 2, 1771, of
John and Eunice (Stoddard) Comstock, he engaged
in a sea-faring career early in life and began preaching in 1800. Among the ship captains of the famous
port that was his native city the name of Comstock
is an honored one. The founder of the Comstock
family in New London County was William, the " old
goodman " who was associated (1650) with John
Winthrop in the building of the corn-mill and dam in
New London. He had his home on Post Hill near
the corner of Williams and Vauxhall Streets. Elkanah's father, John, was first lieutenant in Colonel
Selden's regiment in the Revolutionary War and was
killed in the Battle of White Plains. His grand-
father, John, was appointed to keep a ferry to
Groton in 1740 and in 1746 was Captain of Third
Company, New London.[6]

Elkanah Comstock's first pastorate was in Albany
County, New York. When appointed by the New
York Missionary Convention to serve as a missionary
in Michigan Territory he was preaching in Cayuga

[6] *Comstock Genealogy: Descendants of William Comstock of New
London, Conn.* Edited by Cyrus Ballou Comstock. The Knickerbocker
Press, New York, 1907.

County, New York. By training and disposition he
was amply fitted to become a religious leader on the
frontier. He was a man of " rare practical wisdom,
soundness in faith and fearless fidelity in advocating
it," records a writer in the Baptist Encyclopædia.
" He was prized as a citizen and his home was a
model of well-ordered Christian life."

To Elkanah and Sally (Green) Comstock were
born eleven children, some of whom settled in Michigan to become useful in their respective communities. The second child, Elias, moved to Owosso in
1836, where he became Associate Judge of the Circuit Court and for forty years served as a deacon
in the Baptist church of Owosso.

What salary the church paid " Elder " Comstock
on his arrival in Pontiac we do not know as the
earliest records of the church have been lost, but on
April 14, 1828, the church voted to pay him one hundred dollars, " one-third of the amount to be in cash,
the rest in produce." In 1831 declining health compelled Mr. Comstock to resign the pastoral charge
of the church. Two years later he returned to New
London, Connecticut, where he died May 13, 1834.

A powerful revival of religion swept Pontiac in
1837 and among the prominent citizens converted
was no less a personage than Abner Davis, the man
who helped his wife across Clinton River the night
of Baptist beginnings fifteen years before. A few
weeks later Abner was among the first to contribute
$200 for the erection of a Baptist meeting-house on
a lot given to Orisson Allen by the Pontiac Company

for the benefit of the church of which he was one of the charter members. The lot was deeded to the church by Allen and his wife February 26, 1839.

IV

THE GOSPEL IS BROUGHT TO MICHIGAN
INDIANS

I. The First Baptist Missionary to Michigan
Indians

Elon Galusha, who assisted in forming the first
Baptist Church of Pontiac in 1822, was not the first
ordained Baptist minister to enter Michigan, whose
coming to the then territory is a matter of historical
record. In February, 1821, Isaac McCoy, who at the
time was a missionary to the Miami Indians at Fort
Wayne, Indiana, under appointment by the Baptist
Board of Foreign Missions, visited Detroit to interview Governor Cass. Many difficulties had arisen
at his mission, financial and otherwise, and it was
necessary for McCoy to exert himself almost beyond
human endurance to keep the enterprise going. At
a critical hour he received word that Governor Cass,
of Michigan Territory, would receive him and possibly extend government aid. In the dead of winter
McCoy made the long trip on horseback. The journey to Detroit and return to Fort Wayne was accomplished successfully during February and March,
1821. Isaac McCoy's account [1] of this pilgrimage,
and a later one to Ohio, is of great historic interest

[1] *History of Baptist Indian Missions*, by Isaac McCoy. New York,
1840.

to Michigan Baptists because the Fort Wayne mission was transferred to Niles, Michigan, in 1822.

TWO WINTER PILGRIMAGES TO SAVE A MISSION

BY ISAAC McCOY

Amidst the anxieties which poverty, under our peculiar circumstances, was calculated to produce, a worthy Presbyterian brother, a Mr. Hudson, an entire stranger to us, wrote from Detroit, that if we were in great need, he thought, that by a visit to that place, I might, possibly, obtain assistance from Government. As might be supposed, we were not long in deciding what to do. In company of the mail-carrier, I set out for Detroit (two hundred miles), on the eighteenth of February. We spent the first night in a deserted Indian camp, where, by the light of our fire, I made the following note, which I find in my journal: "My mind is oppressed with anxiety. We are deeply in debt. Our wants have long since, and often, been made known to the board, but no relief has arrived. The situation of our affairs never appeared more precarious than at the present. Old debts are becoming due, while necessity compels us to contract new ones, and, should we not obtain relief soon, our mission must be broken up."

On reaching Detroit, my business was with Governeur Cass, who listened to the story of our wants with the sympathy that does honor to humanity, and having control of some public means, he was so kind as to promise me aid. He furnished about four hundred and fifty dollars' worth of clothing and food for our Indian scholars; the latter was in the form of rations for the Indians, and the money for the former was afterwards placed in my hands, so that we might lay it out to the best advantage, which we did in purchasing at the cheapest rate in Ohio. . .

At camp, March 3, I made the following note in my journal: " I have traveled all day along a small trace through the wilderness, have seen no one except four Indians. My own horse having failed before I left the settlement, I hired another to ride, while I led mine. Much wearied with the day's travel, and afflicted with pain in my face, I have just finished my supper, tied up my horses to trees, and now sit alone by a little fire in the wilderness, where I make this note: 'A ride the following day, of twenty miles, under a continual fall of rain, brought me home. The amount received from Government at this time was a very great help for the future, but it afforded no present relief in liquidating debts which we had already contracted, the payment of which could not be delayed. . .' "

On the fifteenth of March our necessities compelled me to set out upon another unpleasant journey over very bad roads, and through snow and rain, to Ohio. But by far the most unpleasant part of the business was that of again asking Mr. Phillips (of Dayton) to lend me money, before I had paid up my old debts to him. He was a humane gentleman, and sympathized with me, but hesitated to risk any more upon the patronage of the board, but desired me to call again. The following note in my journal describes part of the exercises of my mind the following night:

"Spent the night in painful anxiety; reviewed my Christian experience, my call to the ministry, my exercises of mind on the subject of missions, my motives and my hopes, and the dealings of Providence under various circumstances. Has God, thought I, who has preserved my life, and in some instances almost miraculously, who has made me sensible of my unworthiness and of my dependence upon him, who has comforted me often by teaching me to trust in him, and who has given me such an earnest desire to spend the only life which I have to live in this world in a way well-pleasing to him, and who has taught me to pray that I might not materially err from the path of duty—suffered me to engage in the mission and to continue in it so long, and yet not required these labors at my hands? Have all my warm feelings on the subject been delusive? Have the prospects among the Indians brightened merely to confirm the delusion, to lead me further from the right way, and to complete my downfall?" Never did I more earnestly beg, really beg, that God would save us from ruin, if he delighted in our course; and if the way was displeasing to him, to correct us in mercy, and set us right, without allowing any material injury to grow out of our errour.

Agreeably to Mr. Phillip's request, I waited on him again, and told him, plainly, that while I hoped the board would pay the debt that I wished to contract by borrowing, they were under no promise to me to do so. That if they should not choose to allow my accounts, I should not be able to pay him soon; though one day, but not in time to suit his convenience, I should pay him. My wife and I had consecrated our lives and labours to the improvement of the conditions of the Indians; and all that we held dear on earth was, in some degree, connected with this enterprise. If he could risk a loan of money under such doubtful circumstances, he might be the means of saving all; but, if not, I could perceive no way to prevent all from being plunged into ruin in the course of a few weeks. He very generously loaned me money to meet our immediate wants. I never borrowed upon interest. Matters were afterwards so arranged that he was not a loser by his kindness.

II. LEONARD SLATER—WHO GAVE HIS YOUTH

At twenty-four years of age Leonard Slater, of Worcester, Massachusetts (born November 16, 1802), received an appointment to join Isaac McCoy in the Michigan wilderness as a missionary to the American Indians. The year was 1826. With his wife he set out in September, 1826, from his New England home on the long and difficult journey to the Carey Indian Mission Station located near the present site of Niles, Michigan.

After leaving Albany the young couple pursued their journey on the Erie Canal to Buffalo in a freight-boat; traveling night and day (Sundays excepted), they reached Buffalo nine days later. They went by stage to Erie, Pennsylvania, where they took passage on a steamboat for Detroit and arrived there two days later. Directly upon their arrival they presented a letter of recommendation to Francis P. Browning [2] who received them cordially into his family, to wait for the arrival of a guide with saddle horses from Carey. With some degree of impatience they waited two weeks. Then with expressions of gratitude to Mr. Browning and his family for their hospitality they set out on their arduous horseback trip through the wilderness.

The party was nine days traveling from Detroit to Niles (Carey Mission) experiencing wet and cold weather. At night they spread their blankets on the inhospitable ground.

Breaking out of the woods into a clearing one day the Slaters looked out over the Kalamazoo Valley and saw a village nestling beside the river. In this settlement, that later became the city of Kalamazoo, there was only one white man, a French trader by the name of Numaiville. Slater was so delighted with the valley that he said that some day he would like to come back to it. On September 27 they reached Carey and were received cordially by the missionaries there. At the station were Indians, French, and Americans, about eighty people in all, sixty of whom were Indian boys and girls who had been gathered from among the Potawatomi and Miami tribes for Christian instruction.

In 1827 Slater was transferred to Thomas Station

[2] See chapter " Spirit of Our Pioneering Fathers " for sketch of F. P. Browning of Detroit.

(now Grand Rapids), where he remained nine years, teaching and preaching. He learned the Ottawa language so as to use it as readily as English. The Indians became greatly attached to him, and under his teaching many of them became converts to the Christian religion, among whom was the famous Chief Noonday. Isaac McCoy was the founder of Thomas Indian Mission Station; consequently one of the founders of Grand Rapids and has been so regarded by its historians.

The progress of white settlements made necessary a change of residence for the missionary, and in 1836 he removed to Barry County, near Prairieville, where he purchased eighty acres of land and founded a mission and a school for the Ottawas known as Slater Station, which he maintained for the next sixteen years.

To the limit of his power Slater furthered the welfare of the Indians by preaching and teaching and tried in every way possible to shield them from the exploitations of the greedy, rum-selling white men.

In 1852 Leonard Slater moved to Kalamazoo and rode horseback from this point to his Indian field in Barry County. He also preached to the Indians on the streets of Kalamazoo, and Mrs. Slater taught a Sunday school class of Indian children under the trees that now adorn Bronson Park.

When the Indians had been removed Slater devoted himself to the Negroes of Kalamazoo. When he died in Kalamazoo on April 27, 1866, the pioneers for miles around mourned the loss of a great man— one who had lived worthily and had left behind him a memory and example of unselfish living and undying courage. He was buried in Riverside Cemetery, near the spot where he stood in 1826 when he caught his first view of the beautiful Kalamazoo Valley. His last utterance was " Bury me by the Kalamazoo, on the spot where I first spread my tent and slept by the Indian trading-post, on the night of my coming to the Mission."

Slater from the beginning of the movement that resulted in the founding of Kalamazoo College, in 1833, exhibited a genuine interest in the school. When the Baptists of Michigan realized that they must come to the support of the institution and forty acres of land were purchased on the west side of the village, a few individuals—John P. March, S. H. Ransom, Thomas W. Merrill and Leonard Slater being among them—contributed a sum sufficient to pay for the purchase of the land.

III. ABEL BINGHAM, " FATHER " TO THE OJIBWAYS

During five years Abel Bingham had been serving as a missionary among the Seneca Indians on the Tonawanda Reservation in Western New York, under the Baptist Misisonary Convention of the State of New York. Through correspondence with Isaac McCoy he became convinced that he should go to the Ojibway Indians at Sault Sainte Marie, in the Michigan Territory. In the course of time a letter was received by him from Dr. Lucius Bolles, corresponding secretary of the Baptist Board of Foreign Missions, dated " Boston, July 17, 1828." Portions of

GRAVE OF LEONARD SLATER
Kalamazoo, Michigan
Rev. John Frost, Crow Indian, standing at right

that letter are given below because they reflect the fine spirit with which this Board maintained missions among American Indians from their inception until 1865, when missions among the "Aborigines of this country" were transferred to The American Baptist Home Mission Society.

" Reposing great confidence in you as a Christian and one whom the Lord has called to preach his gospel," wrote Doctor Bolles, " the Baptist Board of the General Convention did on the 15th instant, appoint you a missionary to labour among the Aborigines of this country, a service to which you have already been devoted for more than five years in the employ of a sister society in the State of New York. . .

" You are instructed to lose no time in repairing to the Sault Sainte Marie, the scene of your future toils. When arrived there you will call on Henry Schoolcraft, Esq. (U. S. Indian Agent), and confer with him on the subject of locating the establishment proposed and on the best means of carrying the Benevolent intentions of Government into execution, in relation to the Indians. It is understood that the Treaty under which you act has secured to the uses of the Mission one section of land, which you will locate, not interfering with the rights of others, and let any building or buildings which you may erect for your accommodation, and for school and other instruction, be on the said premises. The measure of cultivation and improvement of the soil by you, must depend on circumstances yet to be developed.

" You will take all due measures to conciliate the esteem and confidence of the natives with a view to usefulness among them; will as early as possible commence a school for the instruction of their children and combine with literary, their moral improvement. You will establish and maintain regular Christian worship on every Lord's day for the good of all within the reach of your influence, and should an interpreter be necessary in a part or all the services, you will employ one on the best terms. You will keep a regular journal of your proceedings, which must always be liable to the inspection of this Board, and once every three months transcribe and forward to them the whole thereof, or such parts as shall enable them to form a fair and true estimate of your labours and their results. . .

" That which is most of all important remains yet to be said: ' *Take heed to yourself, and to the doctrine.*' You are about entering upon duties involving the interests of immortal souls for eternity, and they cannot be successfully discharged without God.

" Maintain the life piety in your own heart—be often at the throne of grace—watch over your tempers, words and actions—grieve not the Holy Spirit of God. Dwell among the natives as a Father, exercising all gentleness and kindness among them, that if possible you may win them to the living God, and in the day of the Lord Jesus have them for the crown of your rejoicing. Use all diligence in the prosecution of your work, knowing that the time is short.

" So far as aught in these instructions may be applicable to Mrs. Bingham as your amiable partner, and who is ultimately expected to be associated with you at the Mission Station, we wish her to receive the same, with ardent desire on our part for your usefulness and happiness."

From Bingham's unpublished *Journal* that is kept in the archives of the American Baptist Foreign Mission Society, exact copies have been made for this volume of the entries covering Bingham's trip by water from Buffalo to Sault Sainte Marie. He spent a total of seventeen days on board two schooners traveling from one end to the other of Lake Erie and Lake Huron. Today on the fastest steamships one can cross the Atlantic Ocean nearly four times during the same period. Bingham's brief daily record is illuminating, affording us an insight into the character of the man who had been entrusted with the responsibility of opening the first Baptist mission in the Upper Peninsula.

" Monday, Sept. 8th, 1828—Took an affectionate leave of my dear family & friends, started my journey for the St. Maries, with a view to spending a few days at Tonawanda, in arranging some business at that place. Found the missionary brethren there all sick.

" Saturday 13th—Arrived at Buffalo, found the schooner (Lady of the Lakes) freighted for Mackinaw & Greenbay. Supposing Mackinaw was directly on my way, went immediately on board and engaged my passage to that place—Put up with Br. Smith with the design of spending the Sabbath with him—In the morning the wind having shifted the vessel put out; of course had to spend my Sabbath on the Lake. After breakfast all hands were invited into the cabin, save those employed in managing the vessel, for worship. In the afternoon, wind being high, lake rough, was seasick. Was detained at Sandusky bay by contrary wind two days.

" 20th. Arrived at Detroit, yet out of health—

" Lord's Day 21st—Unable to preach.

" Attended a funeral, 22nd.

" 23rd. Tried to preach in the evening at the Methodist meeting house—On arriving at Detroit I was informed Mackinaw was 40 or 50 miles out of my way, & was advised by friends to stay at that place until a vessel should arrive that was bound to the Sault—Accordingly I tarried ten days, put up with Br. F. T. Browning, who on my arrival very generously invited me to make myself at home at his house. Here I was treated with great kindness, had opportunity to form an acquaintance with some interesting friends, among whom was a Mr. Phineas Davis & his Lady who entered deeply into the subject of missions, and you know Sir, such friends are doubly dear to missionaries. My health continued poor, yet I tried to preach on the Sabbath—28th.

" 29th—Monday morning—Had an interview with Governeur Cass on the subject of my mission.

"30th—The Schooner John Adams, arrived on her way to the S. St. Maries—I went on board, sailed at 12 o'clock at night.

" Oct. 2nd—Being obliged to lie at anchor in the St. Clair River, in the evening went on shore & preached, it being a new destitute place.

" Oct. 4th—Got into Lake Huron, soon had a smart gale, was seasick.

" 5th—Lord's Day—Rough sea, sick all day, obliged to keep my berth——

" 7th—Lying at anchor under cover of Drummonds' Island, the Capt. called all hands into the cabin for worship—I read, prayed and gave them an exhortation—My health now improving.

" 8th—Weighed anchor, got underway, had a pleasant time.

" 1828—Oct. 9th. At half past 8 in the evening, anchored at the Sault De St. Marie—Never felt myself under greater obligation, and very seldom esteemed it a greater privilege, to bless & praise God for his goodness to me, than at this time. As we had had prayers regularly on board the vessel when I was able to attend to it, on our arrival the Capt. called all hands into the cabin, for worship. I was directed to the 66th Ps.—It seemed that we all felt a peculiar pleasure in offering tribute of praise to God—After prayer I read the sailor's address, (a hymn which I had written about sons of the main, etc.) On learning that the Capt. was pleased with it, I presented it to him, together with a couple of tracts, which he received with pleasure. I also distributed some Tracts among the men—As also I did to Capt. Walker & his men, on Board the Lady—

"Oct. 10th—Sault De St. Marie—Early this morning went on shore—Called on Mr. Schoolcraft U. S. Agent, by whom I was kindly received, & with whom I breakfasted and dined—After breakfast I went in company with Mr. Schoolcraft to visit the Rev. Mr.

Coe a Presbyterian brother who has been labouring here for more than a year, under many disadvantages, who together with his lady, appear extremely anxious to build up Zion.—Br. Coe in particular seems much devoted to Indian reform, Sister Coe has for a short time taught a school here, until she was obliged to relinquish it, on account of her health. Br. Coe has since collected the Indian children, an hour or two in a day, and taught them, some in English, some in Indian.— (But they expect to leave here, by the first vessel that comes to the place)— Spent the rest of the day in making necessary enquiries—Found that the land granted to government, for the military establishment, covers all the village & houses, of course a house must be rented for school—Learned that house rent, & board, were very high—

" 11th—Spent most of Thursday in writing letters as the Adams is to sail this evening.

" 12th—Lord's day—Preached at Mr. Coe's place of worship from John 10: 10 last clause—At 2 P M went in company with Mr. Coe to attend his meeting with the native children—Some females attended. . . In the evening attended a prayer meeting at our place of worship, which was quite interesting——

This evening, had my first interview with an Ojibway Indian, one of the minor chiefs, (& as I was informed by the Agent) a pipe bearer to the principal chief—I informed him, that, in compliance with the arrangements made in the Treaty at Fondulack [Fon du Lac]. I had come to establish a school for the instruction of their children, and to preach the *gospel* of the *Lord Jesus* unto them. He said he was very glad I had come, for he had three children he wished to send to school. I also gave him some instruction on the subject of religion and requested him to think candidly on the subject, & inform me how he liked it—He replied, that, as he was going to start for his hunting ground tomorrow, he should not be able to return to inform me now, but when he returned in the winter he would then let me know, his mind on the subject."

In the following spring Bingham returned to his home in Wheatland, New York, where he was ordained. Returning to Sault Sainte Marie with his family, he opened a school, cleared some land and built a mission house in the summer of 1829. During the twenty-seven years he remained at his station he suffered many discomforts and perils, often making extended trips in the winter on snow-shoes and with dog-teams. His school was maintained almost continuously. He established a church for the Indians that in 1833 reported fifty-five members, including soldiers. His familiar title "Father Bingham" was an evidence of the affectionate regard with which whites and Indians held him. Upon the scattering of the Indians in 1855 he went to Grand Rapids to live with his children. He died in 1866.

Baptist Trail-Makers in Michigan

V

WOMANHOOD'S GIFT TO THE MICHIGAN FRONTIER

In 1822 Isaac McCoy and Christiana, his wife, with their children and a few helpers, transferred their missionary headquarters from Fort Wayne, Indiana, to Michigan and established near the present site of the city of Niles a school for Indian boys and girls that became known as the Carey Mission. The Daughters of the American Revolution have erected on the site of that vanished mission a memorial of bronze and granite to Isaac McCoy. Not far from Niles is a beautiful body of living, crystal water about which people have built summer homes and a recreational park. It is called Lake Christiana in honor of the memory of the courageous wife and mother without whom Isaac McCoy would have been helpless to accomplish all that he did in behalf of the American Indian. The writer has chosen to insert here a story about this pioneer woman, written by a woman, that deserves wide reading. We present as a toast " Christiana McCoy, Heroine of the Michigan Wilderness " [1] to those who are celebrating one hundred years of Baptist achievement in Michigan.

[1] From *Missionary Pioneer Heroines in America,* by Anna Canada Swain. Used by permission of Department of Missionary Education of the Board of Education of the Northern Baptist Convention.

Baptist Trail-Makers in Michigan

A WOMAN PAYS TRIBUTE TO THE MEMORY OF A PIONEER WOMAN OF MICHIGAN

By Anna Canada Swain

In the latter part of the eighteenth century women were not considered very important. Their husbands *did* things and a record was kept of *their* achievements, but when it came to the women, the only record of importance seems to have been the date of marriage. So far as we can find, there is no account anywhere of the date of Christiana Polk's birth. We know that her husband, Isaac McCoy, was born in Pennsylvania in 1784 and that they were married in 1803 when *he* was nineteen. She was the daughter of a Captain Polk whose wife and several children had been captured by the Ottawas. By a strange coincidence she was destined later to be a missionary to that very tribe which had carried away her mother.

Although most of the records are of Isaac McCoy and his accomplishments, in his diary he continually speaks in most loving appreciation of what his wife meant to him and his work. Some have thought he was hard-hearted because he allowed his wife to be without him when five of their children died. It is hard to see how any one could feel this if he sensed at all the earnestness with which this great missionary strove to better the condition of the much neglected Indian people. He loved his own family dearly but he felt that he was practically alone in realizing the great injustice which was being done a conquered race, and that if he did not act, no one would.

In 1804, the young couple moved to Indiana, where they had a remarkable influence on the churches. Every great cause of the denomination was supported to the best of their ability. It was not until 1810 that Isaac was ordained and 1817 when he received an appointment as missionary to the Indians of Indiana and Illinois.

The life which Christiana McCoy was called on to live was unbelievably hard. The old records are full of accounts of serious illnesses, accidents, cold, hunger, lack of money, and danger; but she was evidently a real pioneer for when the need arose—as it did repeatedly—she became the efficient head of the mission, often for weeks at a time. If her husband were too ill to attend to some important matter, she did not hesitate to mount a horse and with her youngest baby in her arms ride forth on the errand herself. On at least one such occasion she was obliged to camp out in the forest alone at night. She must have had great dignity along with her courage, for her husband once remarked that the Indians were very respectful in her home and they were not in many white homes.

Very early in their career the McCoys discovered that the best way to have a real influence and to accomplish their object was to take Indian children into their home. This would have been an excellent move had Baptists realized the importance of the work being done and supported it. Unfortunately there was a large group of churches, especially in that part of the country, which was definitely anti-missionary. In addition to that, the board did not pay the McCoys until after expenses had been incurred and there must have always been a dread on their part that the Board might not approve and hence might not pay at all. The cost of living was very high in the frontiers of those days and it was an expensive proposition to feed and clothe a family of twenty or more.

At times their furniture was so meager and poor that Mrs. McCoy was even ashamed to have the Indians see it, and more than once she felt that the clothing of their little pupils was so ragged that they could not possibly have the right influence with neighboring Indians. And yet they kept on, moving farther away from civilization as the Indians retreated before the relentless white man.

On May 3, 1820, the McCoy family started for a new work in Fort Wayne, where they intended opening a school. There lay before them a tract of country where few white people had ever been. Six Indian children, who had been living in their home, accompanied them and eighteen or twenty other Indians went along to help with their live stock and to put their children in the new school. They drove with them fifteen head of cattle and forty-three swine. At one of the first Indian villages to which they came, their whimsical helpers all deserted them and they found themselves without guides or helpers and with no money to hire any.

Mr. McCoy and Mr. Lykins, realizing that the situation was serious, left Christiana and her children in a clearing and went ahead to explore. They found a village whose insolent drunken inhabitants

ISAAC and CHRISTIANA McCOY

First Baptist Missionaries in Michigan

had never before seen either cattle or whites. They managed to escape, though with difficulty, and tried with very little expectation of help to send a message through the lines to a friendly chief. That night Isaac wrote in his diary what had happened during the day and then carefully hid the book away so that his wife would have no suspicion of the danger they were in. The next day the two white men again went out to explore, hoping to find some way past the hostile village. While they were gone, our heroine discovered the diary and had a good laugh at her husband for trying to conceal it from her. But almost by a miracle the message did go through and they were escorted safely by the dangerous place.

Finally after eleven days of disagreeable rain and real danger they reached Fort Wayne. The nearest white settlement was one hundred miles away. On May 29, 1820, the new school opened with ten American, six French, one Negro and eight Indian pupils. Despite the fact that there were again twenty to supervise in her family, Mrs. McCoy instructed Indian women in knitting and other domestic tasks and also labored especially to convert the women. She was very successful along this line and two of the most influential half-breed women of the town were baptized at a most touching service.

By August Mrs. McCoy was so worn out that her husband urged her to take a little vacation trip to Ohio. She returned at the end of fifteen days to find her five children very ill with bilious fever, a

misfortune which must have discouraged the taking
of vacations.

More and more opportunities came to enroll Indian pupils, and no matter how much illness or work
there was, this dauntless woman could not resist
adding to her family. By September she had added
six more pupils and in November the number was
thirty. Money had not come from the board as they
had expected, and they were deeply in debt. They
were very cold at night and all that there was left
to eat was hominy.

In desperation Mr. McCoy started for Ohio. He
knew very few people there, but he could not stand it
any longer to see his family so undernourished and
worried. He went to a leading merchant in Dayton,
Mr. Horatio G. Phillips, a man whom he did not
know at all, and was most kindly received. He ex-
plained the situation and with Mr. Phillips' aid, he
was able to purchase " three cows, a fresh supply of
flour, and pork and paper, etc., for the school, and
other articles needed " and to "hire a female to
assist in domestic labors." With joyful heart he
returned to his discouraged family. Mr. Phillips
had saved the mission. By the end of 1820 there
were thirty-two Indians in the school.

The following June Mrs. McCoy was in need of
medical attention. Leaving Mr. McCoy in charge,
she took with her three younger children. In an
open canoe they went between three and four hundred miles down the Wabash, more than half the distance through wild country inhabited by totally un-
civilized Indians. It was at a time when the weather

was very hot and rainy, and by the time they reached civilization their clothes were badly mildewed. The mosquitoes were very troublesome. On September 14, the little party returned, bringing with it a new baby which had been born while they were away. Isaac McCoy was very thankful to see them for more than one reason. The school had by that time grown to forty-eight pupils, and he realized how very heavy was the task which he often had to call on his wife to undertake.

In 1822, when a few helpers were added to the missionary staff, a set of agreements was drawn up. The one headed " seven " seemed unnecessary considering the way Mrs. McCoy had always worked. It read:

> " 7. We agree that agreeably to their strength and ability all the female missionaries should bear an equal part of the burden of domestic labours and cares, lest some should sink under the weight of severe and unremitted exertions."

Again in 1822 the mission was moved, and this time even farther away to a spot near Niles, Michigan. The new station they called Carey after the great English missionary. Mr. McCoy must have left much of the management of this station to his wife, for he himself traveled far and wide trying to interest people in his work. Some of his trips were to Washington where, as an authority on Indian affairs, he gave expert advice. Other trips were made to raise money. At times when he ate at well-ladened tables in the East, he sickened as he thought

E   [53]

how at home they so carefully had to portion out the morsels of food.

The work at Carey was most successful. The baptisms were many, but Mr. McCoy records that the greatest obstacle to his work was the introduction of whisky to the Indians by the white man. He labored earnestly in Washington to make Congress see that the only way to Christianize the Indian was to give him his own land where he could be protected from the unscrupulous whites who sought to exploit him.

In November, 1826, the McCoys gave up the personal superintendence of the Carey Mission and moved west to explore and select suitable Indian lands. That one-hundred-twenty-mile journey was one of the most dangerous which they ever took. There were thirteen people in their caravan. They had a one-horse wagon, five horses, and twenty-three swine. They hired an ox-team to carry hay and provision as far into the wilderness as it dared to go. It was a trackless snowy region. The ox-cart mired and was with great difficulty extricated. Later the wagon upset on a hill and Mrs. McCoy and four of the children were pinned underneath. The baby was breathless when pulled out, but was finally revived. They lost their way in the piercing wind, about which time the baby developed a bad fever. They finally pulled through, however, though very much the worse for the experience.

The knowledge Mr. McCoy was obtaining was continually necessitating trips to Washington. By 1840 he published his *History of Baptist Indian Missions,* a volume which is full of interesting material and has been much consulted. In 1842 the American Indian Mission Association was formed and Isaac McCoy was made secretary with headquarters at Louisville, Kentucky.

Although we find no record of it, we hope that from that time Mrs. McCoy had an easier time. Four years later her husband died very suddenly from exposure in a storm. Six years later our heroine, too, died. As was typical of those early records, very little attention was paid to women no matter what they did. In a little volume purporting to be a memorial to Reverend and Mrs. McCoy, even the date of her death (1851) is mentioned only in a footnote and no details are given. Despite this fact, she was appreciated. One biographer says, " There was but one Isaac McCoy—with the best of wives at his right hand."

VI

SPIRIT OF THE FRONTIER

I. Squire Manro

Mention has been made of the coming to Pontiac, in 1818, of Orisson Allen, a Baptist layman, and his family.

Record should now be made of the journey to the Michigan wilderness of another Baptist layman named Squire Manro, whose purpose in coming was not to take up land nor to establish a home but to discover at first hand the religious needs of the new settlements. This man was a prosperous farmer living in Camillus, Onondaga County, New York. At his own expense he came. The year was 1822 (or the early part of 1823). His report coupled with that of Elon Galusha materially furthered the cause of Christ on the frontier. The name of Deacon Squire Manro will be held in grateful memory as long as Baptist institutions exist in Michigan. When account is taken of the difficulties of travel in those early days, the remoteness of the Michigan wilderness, the needs of the growing communities in his own State and his advanced age, the wonder is that Squire Manro was able to accomplish what he did for the Baptist cause in the territory toward which the tide of emigration had turned. But he made the trip, and as the first president of the newly formed Baptist Missionary Convention of the State of New

York he made his report. The Convention at its
second annual meeting, convened at Vernon, Oneida
County, October 15 and 16, 1823, recorded its appreciation of the missionary journey of the venerable
Baptist layman as deserving of notice. The Convention Board in its report for 1823 stated that
Squire Manro " found the Territory in great moral
darkness, very much needing the labor of missionaries, and presenting the most favorable openings,
where the people are desirous to receive the embas-
sadors of Christ."

Squire Manro was born in Rehoboth, Massachusetts, June 27, 1757.[1] His great-grandfather, John,
emigrated from Scotland in the early settlements of
America.

At the commencement of the Revolutionary War,
when eighteen years of age, he entered the service
of his country and continued in the army three
years. After struggling several years to support a
family on small rented farms in Massachusetts, he
moved to Western New York and acquired land
when it was cheap. His deep interest in religious
affairs began soon after his marriage, in 1778, to
Mary Daggett, a great-granddaughter of Col. Ben-
jamin Clark, who won fame as an officer in King
Philip's War. Both were faithful in the practice
of Christian stewardship and took a deep interest in
the benevolent objects of the day. In addition to
the generous gifts to the local Baptist church which
he helped to build, he contributed regularly to for-

---

[1] *Historical Sketch of the Baptist Missionary Convention of the State
of New York,* by John Peck and John Lawton. 1837.

eign and home missions. Ministerial education early received his attention.

Squire Manro was nearly sixty-six years of age when he undertook the long journey to Michigan at about the time the laymen and women at Pontiac were getting Michigan's first Baptist Church under way. Michigan ·Baptists may well cherish his name in grateful memory. In the life of this devoted layman we see exemplified the soul of such an organization as the New York Baptist State Convention that made its contribution to the needs of the growing frontier ten years before the formation of The American Baptist Home Mission Society.

II. FRANCIS P. BROWNING

In the life sketches of Leonard Slater, of the Thomas Mission (Grand Rapids), and of Abel Bingham, the pioneer Baptist of Sault Sainte Marie, in this volume, it will be noted that both of these men, when they passed through Detroit (Leonard in 1826 and Bingham in 1828) on the way to their respective fields of labor, were entertained at the home of Francis P. Browning. In their journals both referred to this Detroit merchant in terms of highest esteem and gratitude. His was preeminently the type of Christian manhood that brought Michigan's early settlements forward in matters of education, religion and morals. During his brief life in Eastern Michigan he spared neither time nor substance to advance public welfare. "Among the outstanding laymen in these early years. . . Francis P. Browning should be first mentioned," wrote Thomas T. Leete, Jr., in 1926. We append Mr. Leete's reference to the man.

AN OUTSTANDING LAYMAN
By Thomas T. Leete, Jr.

He (Francis P. Browning) was a business man with far-seeing vision. He built the first steam mill in Michigan on the Black River in what is now Port Huron. He was considered one of the constituent members of the First Church of Detroit in 1827, although his church letter from the Pontiac Church was not received in time for the organization. He was designated as the leader in church service for three years, until 1831, while the church was without a pastor. Rev. Samuel Haskell in his historical address in 1852 says of Mr. Browning:

"Brother Browning was accustomed to expound the Scriptures, read public discourses, conduct a Sunday school and exercise a general presidency over the action of the church. Though not solicited by agents, they did not forget to send up their annual contribution to the treasurer of Home & Foreign Missions and tract and Bible organizations. The efforts of Mr. Browning and others placed on the lot (at the corner of Fort and Griswold Streets) a building for the use of the church, of humble dimensions but of precious memory to those whose recollection extended back to the scenes within its walls."

The scourge of cholera appeared in the city in 1832 and the church was again without a pastor and great discouragement prevailed, but Mr. Browning again took the lead and at his own expense went in person to Eastern cities to find a pastor for the little group. He was unsuccessful in his mission, but the church kept its faith and under his leadership completed the new church building—which became a visible monument to his untiring energy, for he died in the cholera scourge that again visited the city in 1834 and was the most fatal of all cholera seasons to the little city. Quoting again from Doctor Haskell:

> "Browning with many of his fellow citizens sank under the stroke of the pestilence as he was hastening to and fro through the wasted and frightened city, striving to put back that stroke from others. The pastor's place, the office of deacon, clerk, Sunday School superintendent and trustee, all of which he filled, were by that one sad blow vacated."

III. JUDGE CALEB ELDRED

The original route for travelers between Detroit and Chicago was over the old Indian trail that penetrated the unbroken wilderness before a settler's cabin had been erected in the Lower Peninsula. The pioneer home-seekers, following this trail to some point of divergence, would then be guided by the blazed trees to their lands.

One of the first Baptist pioneers to settle in Western Michigan was Judge Caleb Eldred, whose name became associated with the promotion of education, temperance, and other worthy movements in the new country. He was born April 6, 1781, in Bennington County, Vermont. In 1802 he married Phœbe Brownell and in the following year moved to Otsego County, New York, where he became engaged in farming and later in cattle buying for the Philadelphia market. He was twice elected to the New York State Legislature. He served his township as justice of the peace. By indorsing too freely the notes of the importunate his fortune was swept away and he was brought to the necessity of borrowing money from a friend in order to make the journey to the Michigan Territory of which he had heard favorable reports. In the summer of 1830, at the age of fifty-one, he set out for the distant region. At the outset he was halted at Jackson (then Jacksonburg) by reason of a severe attack of " fever and ague." But he hired Ruel Starr, whom he had met in Detroit, to continue westward and prospect for land in the unsettled region. Starr returned with a glowing account of the country about Kalamazoo. Upon recovery from his illness Judge Eldred, with Starr as his guide, went on to locate a claim at Comstock and employed Ralph Tuttle to build a log house upon it. (Tuttle's log house for many years was noted as a place where any weary emigrant passing through the region might find rest and food offered with genuine hospitality.) Before the winter set in Judge Eldred returned to New York to help his family prepare for the journey to Michigan. In

January, 1831, he returned with his son, Daniel B., and the two occupied the new house.

Judge Eldred at once observed that one of the greatest needs of the new settlements was a saw-mill and he proceeded to erect one on the stream at Comstock. Before the winter was over he and his son with a team of horses met the rest of the family at Detroit. With the heavy load the return trip was exceedingly difficult. There were bridges over the large streams only as far as Ann Arbor. They found the marshes more difficult to cross than the rivers. The nail-kegs that composed part of the freight could be rolled over the boggy places, but to get the square boxes over the treacherous sink-holes taxed their strength and ingenuity to the utmost. The next season Judge Eldred hauled over the same trail the mill-stones for the first grist-mill in Kalamazoo County except a small one at Vicksburg.

The grist-mill was an unparalleled boon to the households in the new country. The nearest one was at Marshall. Formerly the Indian corn-mill was the only contrivance for grinding grain that was available in the wilderness, other than the tin graters the settlers used. To A. D. P. Van Buren, an early contributor to Battle Creek and Kalamazoo newspapers,[2] we are indebted for a description of the way the primitive Indian corn-mill was constructed: "A long pole or sapling was pinned to a tree like a well-sweep, the lower part of which was pestle-shaped; the top of the stump was hollowed out to hold the corn. The sweep was then worked up and down

[2] *History of Kalamazoo County,* by Samuel Durant, p. 86.

[62]

by one of the squaws, while another steadied and directed the pestle, which, as it came down, mashed the corn in this crude mortar."

One of the vanguards in the educational, religious and social movements of his day, Judge Eldred devoted much of his time in voluntary service for the betterment of society in the new Territory. As soon as the first-comers had built their rude cabins at Comstock he became actively interested in promoting religious worship for the people. " Elder " Thomas W. Merrill, as " the itinerant pioneer preacher in this new region," was in the Territory when Judge Eldred arrived. In the latter's home was held the first religious service in Comstock, and it was conducted by Thomas Merrill. Meetings were held on alternate Sundays at Judge Eldred's house and at Sherman Comings' house on Toland Prairie. When the preacher for any reason failed to put in his appearance the congregation at either place selected someone to read a sermon. These meetings resulted in the organization of the first Baptist Church in Western Michigan. The " conference " that was to determine the formation of this historic body met in the house of Stephen Eldred, February 19, 1832, in the village of Comstock. In the words of the old record (Judge Caleb Eldred was the first clerk)[3] the moderator (Elder Reuben Winchell), presented the following " brethren ": Caleb and Phœbe Eldred, Phœbe Eldred, Clark Hall, Chloe Winchell, Chloe C. Winchell, with their letters of recommendation and dismission.

[3] *History of Kalamazoo County*, by Samuel W. Durant, p. 372.

It was voted by the conference that the new body be known as the First Baptist Conference of Arcadia.

A Committee was appointed to prepare articles of faith and practice to be read to the conference in March. On April 8, 1832, the "articles of faith and practice and covenant," were adopted and the church constituted as the "First Baptist Church of Arcadia." The following persons, with the locations of the churches from which they received letters of dismissal given, composed the charter membership: Caleb Eldred and Phœbe (his wife), Phœbe Eldred, Clark Hall, Butternuts, N. Y.; Chloe Winchell, Chloe C. Winchell, Lockport, N. Y.; Isaac Briggs and Betsey A. Briggs (his wife), admitted December, 1833, Athol, Mass.; Alvin Burdick and Lydia Ann Burdick (his wife), Butternuts, N. Y.; Lewis S. Toby, New Raritan, N. J.; Silas Dunham, Henrietta, N. Y.; Edwin S. Dunham, Rochester, N. Y.; Fannie Marsh, West Towsend, Vt.; Daniel Eldred, New Lisbon, N. Y.; Michael Spencer, Joshua Spencer, Ypsilanti, Mich. Thomas W. Merrill was admitted on September 16, 1832, at which time the church voted to change its name to the First Baptist Church of Comstock. In 1847 the name was changed to the First Baptist Church of Galesburg. The church has no individual corporate existence at present. First Church of Kalamazoo, organized in 1836, is the oldest existing Baptist church in Western Michigan.

Judge Eldred in 1834 sold his interests at Comstock and removed to Climax, where he owned farming lands. Here he resided until his death. To him Michigan Baptists are indebted as Thomas W. Merrill's chief supporter in his fight to secure a charter for Kalamazoo College. Judge Eldred was a member of the Territorial Legislature in 1835 and 1836. He became the first president of the Board of Trustees of Kalamazoo College, an office he occupied for over thirty years. His venerable figure was one of the familiar ones to be seen at the annual commencement exercises.

From Judge Caleb Eldred, as ardent in his zeal in behalf of the destitute regions as any missionary, came an appealing letter to the New York headquarters of the Home Mission Society in 1833, describing conditions on the frontier:

" Permit me to bring to the notice of the Board, through its Secretary, the almost destitute condition of the whole of Western Michigan, comprising a territory of more than one hundred miles from east to west and from fifty to one hundred miles from north to south, with settlements forming in every county, with emigrants from the different States of the Republic and from Europe, bringing with them their different views of religion; a countless train constantly following, with but here and there an individual who careth for his Master's work. I pray you, as you regard the Baptist cause in this growing region, send us able ministers, who will combat the enemy, expose error, and command by their faithfulness and zeal an influence in this cause, give character to our denomination and successfully (under the blessing of heaven) enlarge the borders of Zion."

IV. They Held Out

The past several years will be remembered as particularly trying ones in family, church and community life. There has been a testing of faith during the period that has been a revelation to those who doubted the permanency of the church as an institution. Characters have been molded and enriched as men and women, young and old, have faced heroically the sacrifices necessary to maintain their church life under adverse circumstances, some assuming burdens far beyond what normally should be expected of them. This spirit has animated our churches from the days of our pioneering fathers as the following letters testify:

From Rev. Wm. Pack, Byron, in 1849:

I have not preached as much in this quarter as formerly. I lost my horse, and not being able to get another, I am under the necessity of going on foot. Two sermons at two different stations, with from five to fiften miles travel a day, has been all my health would allow, but whenever I get tired of footing it I think of my Saviour, and then I get new strength and persevere.

From Rev. Wm. Smedner, Hudson, in 1850:

I have been afflicted, a portion of the year, with the prevailing sickness of this country, (chills and fever,) and my wife also has been confined with it; but I have been enabled to occupy my post, every Lord's day, though sometimes obliged to preach when shaking with the ague. Baptist ministers are so scarce in this country, that no one can be obtained as a substitute in case of sickness, and I cannot consent to remain at home, although sick, when I know how great a disappointment those suffer who assemble for worship, from great distances, and find no minister present to preach to them.

From Rev. E. Anderson, Kalamazoo, in 1850:

During the last two months sickness has prevailed to a greater degree than has been known for many years in this region. Whole families and neighborhoods have been prostrated at the same time, giving the country the appearance of one vast hospital. Many have suffered very much, and even died, it is feared for want of ordinary care. For many weeks I have seen nothing of half the members of my church, except upon their sick beds. Many of our most valued brethren and sisters have been brought to the gates of the grave; but I trust that the Lord has heard prayer on their behalf, and is now gradually restoring them.

I have often felt tempted to give up in despondency, but physicians are active and laborious at their posts, and surely medicine for the soul is as urgently demanded as medicine for the body. How blessed the thought too, that the prescriptions of the physician of souls, when followed, are infallible. Self-denying labor will be rewarded upon the same principle, whether in a Michigan " Opening," or in a Burman jungle. A minister here needs to live much in the future, and be willing to sow seed to be reaped by others after he is dead.

It would be illuminating to call the roll of the prominent Baptist churches in Michigan and ask them whether or not they received mission funds in their formative periods. All of the older churches surely would answer " aye " to the question.

Home Mission funds from State or national treasuries granted to churches at a time when they were most urgently in need of help have been fruitful of results far in excess of the meager amounts appropriated. The history of the First Baptist Church in Ann Arbor is of great interest in this connection. The following paragraphs are taken from the report of Rev. Samuel Graves, dated October 1, 1851, and addressed to The American Baptist Home Mission Society (this church undoubtedly also received State aid) :

" I reached this place on the 5th of October, 1848, soon after which, I received appointment from the Home Mission Society. The church then numbered sixty-seven members, and worshipped in a small, incommodious, and badly located house, with no Bible class, and almost no Sabbath School or Library to match. The congregation nearly run down, and the church, itself, rent by dissension. On the whole, everything seemed about as disheartening as it could well be.

" But since that time, (be it recorded to the praise of God, and the timely aid of the Home Mission Society,) we have seen better days. Dissensions have been healed—harmony and brotherly love restored—a good and substantial house of worship 45 by 65 feet has been completed, and neatly furnished with cushions, carpets, lamps, etc.—a large and interesting Sabbath School has been gathered,— something more than 200 volumes of books have been added to its Library—an interesting Bible class has also been sustained for some time, whose blessed fruits are already apparent.

" During the entire three years it has been our unspeakably delightful privilege to repair to the banks of our Jordan, with the willing and rejoicing convert, on the first Sabbath of some two-thirds of the thirty-six months since my appointment, and we have been permitted to enjoy, by the blessing of a covenant-keeping God, almost a constant revival of religion. At our Associational Anniversary, which occurred in May last, we numbered 216—making a net increase of 149 in less than three years. It is the Lord's doings, and marvelous in our eyes. The Home Mission Society has expended on this field during the three years, the sum of only $430. As a church we would here erect our ' Ebenezer ' to God ; and express our heartfelt gratitude to the friends and contributors to the cause of Home Missions, with the hope that we shall soon be able more than to refund our indebtedness to that noble institution."

It is needless to add that this church has contributed to State and national missionary societies, foreign and home, many hundred times the total amount of financial aid it received in the early years of its existence.

VII

PIONEER GOSPEL RANGER OF WESTERN MICHIGAN [1]

While events on the frontier and among the eastern churches a little over one hundred years ago providentially were pointing the way toward the formation of a national home mission society, a young man named Thomas W. Merrill was being trained at his home in Sedgwick, Maine, and in New England educational institutions, to lead out along untried paths as a missionary exercising the functions both of teacher and preacher. He was destined to receive the first commission granted to a missionary by The American Baptist Home Mission Society and to become the founder of Kalamazoo College.

Merrill was a student in the Latin School at Waterville, Maine, in 1820, when George Dana Boardman, Sr., a member of the faculty, was converted and offered himself to the Baptist Foreign Mission Board for missionary service in India. Merrill was profoundly stirred and became one of a group of students to declare a desire to undertake foreign missionary work. During college and seminary years he did not lose sight of this goal, although it fell out that Burma was not to be his field. He was a graduate of Colby College in the Class of 1825

---

[1] From a life sketch of T. W. Merrill published by the author in *Missions*. Used by permission.

and of the Newton Theological Institution in 1828. October 31, 1828, is the date on a small sheet of paper greatly prized by the late George E. Merrill, grandson of Thomas W. Merrill, bearing an inquiry addressed to Rev. D. Sharp, D. D., Boston.

" Reverend Sir," began Merrill in this letter now a century old, " Please to inform me by directing a letter to Sedgwick, State of Maine, whether, or not, I can obtain any assistance from the Massachusetts Baptist Missionary Society, should any be needed, by reason of visiting the destitute churches in Michigan Territory, and spending some months or years with them. I have written to ascertain some particulars from that region. Respectfully yours, T. W. Merrill."

Assistance did not come from the quarter appealed to, doubtless because of restrictions relative to the Society's " means of doing good." But this circumstance did not prevent Thomas Merrill from becoming a missionary of large usefulness. He belonged to a missionary family.

Daniel Merrill, of Sedgwick, Maine, Thomas' father, was the organizer (1803) of the first society in Maine " for Promoting Education of Religious Young Men for the Ministry." [2] The elder Merrill not only was the pastor of one of the most influential churches in Maine but famed for his pioneering, apostolic zeal that led him to take long journeys to

---

[2] Facility in tracing many of the historical events recorded in this chapter was made possible by reason of extended researches made by Arthur Warren Smith of Winchester, Mass., Rev. David T. Magill of Jackson, Mich., and George E. Merrill of New York; letters and manuscripts of Daniel Merrill and Thomas W. Merrill were made available to the author by the late Secretary George E. Merrill.

remote settlements in the Maine wilderness from the Penobscot to the Bay of Fundy. On these pilgrimages he often fell in with Isaac Case, a tireless missionary of the Massachusetts Society. In 1821, as president of the Maine Baptist Convention, Daniel Merrill advocated a plan for the most extended missionary enterprise in the "destitute region, lying from the St. Croix, on our Eastern Boundary, along the most northerly inhabited parts of Maine, New Hampshire, Vermont, New York, Pennsylvania, Ohio, the Michigan Territory generally, and in Indiana and Illinois." Doubtless he little dreamed that ten years later his two sons, Thomas and Moses, would be laboring as missionaries in extreme western sections of that territory.

Daniel Merrill's long fight in defence of the right of religious freedom resulted in the act of the Massachusetts Legislature granting a charter for Waterville (now Colby) College.[3]

The failure to secure aid from the Massachusetts Society, as we have intimated, did not discourage young Thomas. After a brief period as a teacher in Amherst College, he felt that he must respond to the call of the wilderness. Accordingly he secured the right to secure subscriptions for *Mrs. Judson's Memoirs* and the *American Baptist Magazine* and started west, the destitute Michigan "backwoods" being his destination. He arrived in Detroit May 23, 1829, with seven dollars in his pocket.

The first six months of his residence in Michigan

[3] See *An Unknown Chapter of Baptist History,* by Dr. H. B. Grose, in *Missions* for November, 1927.

Territory, Merrill spent in visiting, on foot and horseback, settlements remote from Detroit where the gospel seldom or never had been heard. T. W. Merrill was ordained at Detroit, February 6, 1831. To visit one settlement containing nearly one hundred people and give them "one Lord's day services," he rode horseback one hundred miles, and to make a house-to-house visitation in the district, twenty miles more. He declared afterwards that he did not regret the exertion. During this time he made an excursion into Canada and visited some of the brave little churches near the Detroit River as well as an African settlement for fugitive slaves. Running short of funds, he opened a Select School in the village of Ann Arbor, November 23, 1829, having as an assistant his brother Moses. Through friends he petitioned the Territorial Legislative Council for a charter for a school that should be under Baptist control with a theological as well as an academic department. The petition was refused, but Merrill's activity resulted in the granting of a charter for an academy to be situated in Ann Arbor with a local board of trustees. This institution in after years became the University of Michigan. Merrill was offered the principalship of the new academy, but refused it. Soon thereafter he severed his relations with the Select School, having taught in Ann Arbor about nine months. Moses Merrill and his wife reopened the Select School and conducted it as a rival of the academy until 1831. In 1833 the latter accepted appointment as missionaries to the Otoe Indians in Nebraska.

Thomas Merrill in the fall of 1830 went forth once more as an independent itinerant missionary. In October, he attended by request the conferences in Zanesville, Ohio, that led to the organization of Granville College (Denison University). Upon his return to Michigan Territory he visited Kalamazoo County, where the first settlers had been on their "betterments" about two years. The emigration had been so rapid that many settlements contained from twenty to one hundred families. From Ann Arbor to Kalamazoo on the Washtenaw Trail at that time the houses were forty miles apart and on the Chicago Trail from ten to fifteen.

A section called Prairie Ronde was first visited by Merrill. Here he found about one hundred families, many of which had come in as squatters on Indian land and were, according to his description, "in their habits and manners uncultivated, in their minds much unenlightened and in their morals much depraved." Religious meetings were seldom enjoyed. He visited other prairies, from ten to forty miles distant, and found most of them "similarly situated." Barn-raisings and barn-dances, Sunday horse-races, husking-bees and the inevitable "military days" brought neighborhoods together occasionally. The drinking of much hard liquor was an attending circumstance at most of these gatherings.

Finding on Prairie Ronde no convenient house for public worship, Merrill devoted several weeks in the fall of 1830 to the task of erecting such a building. "In erecting the house," said Merrill in one of his letters, "I found it requisite to become one of the

THOMAS W. MERRILL

proprietors and to incur much fatigue and exposure. After the completion of the house, as the youth enjoyed no means of instruction, I taught a school for a few months, though it afforded a compensation rather more nominal than real; I have also opened and prosecuted a Sabbath school." This was the first meeting-house and schoolhouse in Kalamazoo County.

At this time (1830) Isaac McCoy, pioneer missionary among the Indians at Carey (Niles), Michigan, was vigorously pushing forward, through writings and extensive travels, measures for the removal, through treaty stipulations, of many Indian tribes to the Indian Territory. At the Thomas Mission (Grand Rapids), Leonard Slater was working as a missionary in behalf of the Indians headed by Chief Noonday. When Merrill first came to Prairie Ronde there was but one Baptist minister within one hundred miles of him in addition to the two indefatigable servants of God at the Indian mission stations just named. (Leonard Slater became one of the early supporters of Kalamazoo College, was a trustee and sent his children to this institution.)

After two years' service as a volunteer gospel ranger [4] Merrill again wrote to Doctor Sharp, secretary of the Massachusetts Baptist Missionary Society for assistance. "Lured not by the prospect of gain," he said, "but by the single prospect of usefulness, I set out from the land of my nativity, at my own charges and in the capacity of a volunteer, for

[4] A term applied to traveling evangelists on the New England frontier.

this western waste; and though I have seen privation and toil and trial, I have never regretted the exertion and sacrifice incurred. I have now exceeded by one-half the time I intended to devote to this Territory. I have not received the amount of ten dollars for my services as a public speaker. I have traveled several thousands of miles at my own expense. Yet I cannot be at present fully satisfied that my duty and my God bid me return. I have nearly exhausted what I brought with me and what I have earned as teacher of youth, and now through you I am induced to appeal to the Massachusetts Baptist Missionary Society for aid. . . The prospect in this section is, that in a few years the ministry will be supported."

The letter bore a postscript which in the light of subsequent history deserves notice here. " We have it in contemplation," added Merrill, " to put into operation an Academy and Theological Institution under the direction of the Baptist denomination, to be located as nearly central in the Territory as circumstances will admit, combining manual with mental exercise, and moral with intellectual cultivation."

In September, 1831, Merrill's project for a Baptist school received the endorsement of the Michigan Baptist Association at Pontiac; the following month leading delegates to the New York Baptist Convention approved the plan, after its presentation by Merrill.

An event of far-reaching importance occurred in New York, April 27, 1832, which affected the religious and educational welfare not only of the Michigan Territory but the entire American frontier. On that day a group of Baptist men of prophetic vision formed The American Baptist Home Mission Society. Thomas W. Merrill was present at the meeting. He had opportunity to give vivid and accurate descriptions of conditions in the newly settled communities in the Land Beyond with particular reference to the needs of Michigan Territory. His plan for a school was endorsed by the brethren present and contributions of ten dollars each were received from Jonathan Going, Nathan Caswell, James Wilson, John H. Harris, Byron Green, William Colgate, and E. Withington.

Before Merrill left New York he addressed (May 3, 1832) an appeal to the Executive Committee of the newly formed Home Mission Society in behalf of the needy and promising mission fields in Michigan and on May 11, 1832, the Committee appointed him "missionary of the Society, for 3 months, to labour in (Michigan) Territory." The Minutes of the Society for May 17, 1832, has this item: "The Compensation of Rev. T. W. Merrill for 3 months was fixed at $50."

Merrill returned to his home in Comstock, Michigan, and began with renewed vigor to press the matter of a Baptist school. With the assistance of his fellow townsman, Judge Caleb Eldred, a petition was presented to the Legislature, but it was not until April 22, 1833, that the charter for the Michigan and Huron Institute (Kalamazoo College) was signed by the governor.

Baptist Trail-Makers in Michigan

There developed considerable rivalry between various places, among them being Comstock, Marshall, and Kalamazoo, in the matter of the location of the new school. The village of Kalamazoo (Bronson), newly made the county seat, won the prize.

" In the fall of 1835 the rapidly growing village of Bronson (Kalamazoo) made the decisive bid for the school by subscribing a fund of $2,500 for land and suitable buildings, and to the Rev. Jeremiah Hall should be given chief credit for the choice of Kalamazoo. Arriving at Bronson from Bennington, Vt., in 1835 as a missionary of the American Baptist Home Mission Society, he founded, in the next year, and became the first pastor of, the First Baptist Church. No sooner had he come upon the scene than he learned that the Michigan and Huron Institute was seeking a home in the western part of the Territory and, further, that strong inducements were being offered by Comstock, Prairie Ronde, Marshall, and other villages. At once he saw the strategic opportunity for Bronson and not only undertook to canvass the village for subscriptions to bring the school here but borrowed money in his own name to meet the payments due on the farm which was being purchased for a site. The result was that, what with delayed payment of pledges and the oncoming depression, he was nearly ruined financially. He left Kalamazoo in 1842 to become president of Granville College (now Denison University) and later returned to Kalamazoo to assume the pastorate of the Tabernacle Baptist Church. . .

"Unfortunately not much is known about the first instruction and teachers since the early trustee records have been lost; but it seems clear that some instruction, perhaps more or less informal, was offered as soon as the Institute building was completed in the fall of 1836. . . There is a single item of information relative to the first teacher or principal in a letter written by Jeremiah Hall to John Alden (of Selburn Falls, Mass.) dated July 15, 1837. Hall states that it is 'nearly a year since Mr. Harvey was appointed,' that he is about to resign and that a new principal is needed at once. 'Mr. Harvey,' then, must have been appointed early in the fall of 1836, and though no history or historian of Kalamazoo College has ever mentioned his name, the evidence that he was the first head and instructor is unimpeachable, since the letter referred to is in the original manuscript and is one of the choicest treasures in the centennial collection.

"The first official announcement of organized term instruction, however, was published in the *Kalamazoo Gazette* for March 11, 1837, by the executive committee:

"MICHIGAN AND HURON INSTITUTE

"'The Academic Department of this institution will be opened for instruction on Wednesday, the 19th of April next, under the superintendence of an experienced and well-qualified Instructor, for the accommodation of young ladies and gentlemen. A few young gentlemen can be accommodated with board at its actual cost at the boarding house, and also can be furnished with employment should they wish to defray all, or part of, their expenses by manual labor.'

" The ' experienced and well-qualified instructor ' was doubtless Mr. Harvey but he resigned about the first of July, 1837. . . .

" On March 2, 1836, the name Bronson had been changed to ' Kalamazoo.' Michigan had been admitted to statehood on Janary 26, 1837. And now the name of the Michigan and Huron Institute was altered to ' The Kalamazoo Literary Institute ' by an amendment to the charter approved March 21, 1837. Various other changes were made but the most interesting one reaffirms the implied non-sectarian position of the first charter in explicit terms :

" ' The said Institute and Departments shall be open to all Christian denominations, and the profession of any religious faith shall not be required of those who become students.' " [5]

Thomas Merrill served the college for many years as a trustee. His gift of $10,000 for endowment was unusually large for the day. He had moved in the meantime to Lansing, where he was successful in business although he did not cease his work as an itinerant throughout the State in behalf of benevolent societies. At his death his will was found to have been drawn in favor of the school he founded and which by that time (April 11, 1878) for a

[5] *Centennial History of Kalamazoo College, 1833-1933*, by Charles True Goodsell and Willis Frederick Dunbar. Kalamazoo, Michigan, 1933.

quarter of a century had been enjoying the privileges of a full-fledged college with degree-granting powers.

Daniel D. Merrill, son of Thomas W., born at Comstock, February 16, 1834, was a student at Kalamazoo College from 1851 to 1854 and in 1855 labored as a colporter-missionary in Indiana and Illinois. In 1856 he took up his residence in St. Paul, Minnesota. As member of the First Baptist Church of St. Paul (a tablet in honor of his memory was unveiled by this church after his death), as the first secretary and treasurer of the St. Paul Y. M. C. A. which he helped to organize, as secretary and treasurer of the United States Christian Commission during the Civil War, as treasurer thirty-five years and president four years of the Minnesota Baptist State Convention, this able layman continued during his lifetime to add luster to the name already written into Baptist missionary history.

To the industry and missionary zeal of the late Secretary George E. Merrill, son of D. D. Merrill, was due the conception and effective organization of the Department of Architecture of The American Baptist Home Mission Society. Prior to this undertaking he had revealed his missionary spirit in the organization of mission Sunday schools in St. Paul and Pittsburgh, and later in leading in the reestablishment of the Baptist cause in Annapolis.

Baptist Trail-Makers in Michigan

CHAUNCEY REYNOLDS

VIII

FREE BAPTISTS OF MICHIGAN

On the seventeenth day of October, 1828, Chauncey Reynolds, twenty-three years of age, bought seventy-eight and one-half acres of land in the Township of Plymouth at $1.25 per acre. He had one shilling left. On the thirtieth day of the same month he married Sally Harper. " No partnership," recorded a son from that union seventy-five years later, " ever began with larger capital in manhood and womanhood."

As Chauncey Reynolds became one of the pioneer Free Baptist ministers in the Michigan Territory, one of the founders of Hillsdale College, making the first contribution of over five hundred dollars to the institution and serving on its first Board of Trustees, as nine of the eleven children born to him and his wife Sally (two having died in early childhood), as well as ten grandchildren, were educated in Hillsdale College either before or after its removal from Spring Arbor, as two of their sons, Lorenzo and Elon Galusha,[1] served in the capacity of secretary-treasurer of the college and other sons and daughters and grandsons and granddaughters served the cause of Christ in Michigan and elsewhere in various ways, an account of some of the incidents relating

[1] Chauncey Reynolds undoubtedly named the youngest son after the first Baptist missionary sent to the Michigan Territory by New York Baptists.

to the establishment of this family in the Michigan wilderness should be of interest to Michigan Baptists.

In the winter of 1836-1837, Chauncey Reynolds, having sold his farm in Plymouth, moved with his family and household goods to the Township of Lyons, Ionia County, where he had filed upon land. His brother, Ira A. Reynolds, who had built a log house in this Grand River Valley country the autumn before, generously shared his roof with Chauncey and Sally and their children until their home was built. Three miles away was the river itself; southward nine miles was the village of Portland; westward five miles the village of Lyons; Ionia, the county seat, lay westward twelve miles; and fifty miles westward was Grand Rapids. Lyons, the nearest market, was an important place in that early day, being at the head of navigation. It was quite the center of the State and so well thought of that it ran a close second to Lansing in the contest over the location of the capital when it was removed from Detroit.

Set down in an unbroken forest with not a rod of improved land, no roads but blazed trees, not a fence within miles, no grist-mill or sawmill near, Chauncey Reynolds had reason to declare that he could stand in his doorway and throw an axe beyond the pale of civilization.

The first morning after their arrival the Reynolds' were aroused from sleep by the howling of wolves. In a wide expanse of territory nothing had been raised for man or beast to eat. The single exception was the crop of turnips owned by two men who had come in the year before. They had raised these on the bottom lands in the bend of the river four miles from the Reynolds' homestead. They had them for sale to newcomers and the Reynolds men worked their way through the woods with oxen and wagon to obtain some. When they reached the river they hailed the men on the opposite bank and bought a few bushels of turnips. The roots were brought across the river in a canoe.

There was the problem of wintering a team of oxen for the coming spring work. Could it be done without hay, straw, or grain? These pioneers found a way. They felled basswood trees so that the oxen could browse off the buds. The hungry animals learned to follow into the woods the man with an axe. But in the early spring came a storm that covered the ground with deep snow; following this a sleet that froze into a crust that cut the legs of the oxen. It became impossible either to lead or drive them into the woods. The family then resorted to the expediency of feeding the oxen from the straw-beds. That pair of pale-red, white-faced oxen licked up the last bushel from the last bed in the house.

Chauncey Reynolds, along with his neighbors, began early to raise sheep. The small flocks were thrown together and the neighbors shared the work of herding them. A common sheepfold was built into which the herd was driven every night. It was built in circular form with a bee-hive-shaped thatched roof. Wolves prowled about the fold at night, sometimes climbing upon the roof in desperate attempts to get at the sheep. They entered the barn-yard to worry the cattle. A large gray wolf was trapped by Frances Reynolds, a brother of Chauncey, brought in, lashed to a long pole, and laid down in front of the sheepfold. It must have been a lesson that the wolf never forgot.

The first schoolhouse was built of logs. The roof was of shakes. The fireplace was built of clay with clay hearth and stick chimney. Two horizontal windows lighted the single school room. The desks were wide boards along each wall under the windows. They were supported by pegs driven into two-inch auger-holes in the wall. The benches were slabs, flat sides up, supported by two flaring pegs at each end, with one perpendicular peg in the middle. The one chair was for the teacher.

Religious and educational privileges were pitiably meager. It was a poor time in which to die as there was no preacher to conduct a funeral service, no undertaker to furnish a casket, and no cemetery in which to bury the dead. Except for children too small to work there was scant time spared the young people to attend school except during a few weeks in the dead of winter.

For nearly twenty years the Reynolds family, like their neighbors, lived in a log house so crudely constructed that during a beating storm, the beds, day or night, had to be drawn out from the walls. After a winter storm the snow had to be taken out of the

HOME NEAR HILLSDALE, MICHIGAN

(Inspiration for "Over the Hill to the Poorhouse," by Will Carleton)

Photo by Felger Studios, Hillsdale, Mich., 1935

attic-chamber by the basketful before the fire below was built; otherwise occurred the discomfort of a rainfall from the snow-banks in the attic. Indian pudding (from corn meal) and hasty pudding (from wheat flour), comprised a large part of the diet; game and fish were plentiful when men had time to hunt and fish. Pumpkins for sauce and pies were dried in the autumn in large quantities on racks over the fireplace. Wild plums and crab apples were gathered before fruit trees were cultivated. From the hard-maple groves came the pioneer's sugar and from the wild-bee trees came his honey.

To clear as wide an area of the primitive forest as possible became the goal of each winter's task. It was back-breaking work. The best timber was cut into saw-logs and drawn to the mill and the lumber drawn home. Less desirable lengths were the " rail-cuts " that, hauled into line, were split into rails for fences. The labor of the winter was seen in the countless brush piles and the burning of the new fallow. The new ground was sown to wheat in the autumn following the clearing of the land.

The experiences of Chauncey Reynolds and his family in the Michigan wilderness remind one of the first nineteen couplets of Will Carleton's poem " The First Settlers' Story," one of the many ballads that Hillsdale's famous poet-graduate wrote to immortalize the pioneer builders of the mid-western States.[2]

[2] From *Over the Hill to the Poor-House and Other Poems*, by Will Carleton ; reprinted here by courtesy of Harper & Brothers, New York and London.

Baptist Trail-Makers in Michigan

It ain't the funniest thing a man can do—
Existing in a country when its new;
Nature—who moved in first—a good long while—
Has things already somewhat her own style,
And she don't want her woodland splendors battered,
Her rustic furniture broke up and scattered,
Her paintings, which long ago were done
By that old splendid artist-king, the Sun,
Torn down and dragged in Civilization's gutter,
Or sold to purchase settlers' bread-and-butter.
She don't want things exposed, from porch to closet—
And so she kind o' nags the man who does it.
She carries in her pockets bags of seeds,
As general agent of the thriftiest weeds;
She sends her blackbirds, in the early morn,
To superintend his fields of planted corn;
She gives him rain past any duck's desire—
Then maybe several weeks of quiet fire;
She sails mosquitos—leeches perched on wings—
To poison him with blood-devouring stings;
She loves her ague-muscle to display,
And shake him up—say every other day;
With thoughtful, conscientious care, she makes
Those travellin' poison bottles, rattlesnakes;
She finds time, 'mongst her other family cares,
To keep in stock good wildcats, wolves, and bears;
She spurns his offered hand, with silent gibes,
And compromises with the Indian tribes
(For they who've wrestled with his bloody art
Say Nature always takes an Indian's part).
In short, her toil is every day increased,
To scare him out, and hustle him back East;
Till finally it strikes her, some fine day,
He entered that locality to stay;
Then she turns 'round, as sweet as anything,
And takes her new-made friend into the ring,
And changes from a snarl into a purr:
From mother-in-law to mother, as it were.

Free Baptists of Michigan

Gradually the forest moved back until Chauncey Reynolds' three hundred acres were nearly all improved. In those early days the wheat was cut with a "turkey-wing" cradle, the hay with a scythe. Before there were barns the grain was threshed in open fields with flails or oxen. The routine of farm life was broken by community gatherings that included logging-bees, barn-raisings, corn husking-bees, butchering, sheep-washing and -shearing.

There were spiritual needs in the wilderness to which Chauncey Reynolds responded willingly and to the best of his ability. He became a lay minister, and with other farmer preachers helped to build the foundation of the Free Baptist denomination in Michigan. He was ordained by the Grand River Quarterly Meeting in 1845.

Henry S. Limbocker, answering what he considered to be a divine call, went to Michigan from Parma, New York, in 1830. Landing at Detroit, he walked thirty miles into the country and began to preach the gospel in a neighborhood where no religious services had been held. In 1831 he was ordained by the Bethany (New York) Quarterly Meeting and then returned to Michigan to organize near Ypsilanti the first Free Baptist church in Michigan. Dr. Henry M. Ford, formerly the general secretary of the Free Baptist denomination, has a vivid recollection of Limbocker. Regarding him he told the writer: "His was a craggy countenance like a rock overhanging a mountain. Piercing eyes gleamed beneath shaggy eyebrows. Although uneducated he used good language and made a fine appearance on the platform. He could preach a strong, vigorous sermon."

Elder John Norton had settled in Macomb County in 1826 and helped to form the Oakland Quarterly Meeting in 1832, the year of his death. Three churches made up this first Quarterly Meeting in Michigan—Washington (later Bruce), Ypsilanti, and Farmington Free Baptist churches. In 1833 the Bloomfield, Plymouth, Novi, Pontiac, and Saline churches were added; in 1834 the Huron, Jackson-burgh (later Jackson), Neri, Pitt (later Pittsfield), and Webster churches came in.

Active also in forming some of the earliest Free Baptist churches in Michigan were Elijah Cook and Samuel Whitcomb. In 1835 Cook located at Cook's Prairie, where he recognized the need of religious work and energetically entered into it. Whatever may have been his talents as a preacher, he certainly enjoyed liberty in song. Whitcomb and Cook, traveling and working together, formed a powerful evangelistic team. Whitcomb, being the more effective speaker, was ably supported by Cook, the hymn-singer.

Whitcomb, Cook, and Limbocker, first founders of the Free Baptist denomination in Michigan, like Chauncey Reynolds, of Ionia County, had to work by day on their farms to support their families. Their education had been limited to the narrow bounds of the common district school. Frequently they studied their texts with the Bible in one hand and the bridle in the other as they rode to their appointments. It was not unusual for them to ride twenty miles or more after a Sunday evening service to be at home on Monday morning to begin the week's labor in the fields. They did not always ride. " In one year he (Limbocker) traveled 2,900 miles (all on foot except 125), preached 300 sermons, attended sixty other meetings, and did fully half a man's work in support of his family." [3]

Denied educational advantages in their youth, to their credit it must be said that they became ardent advocates of an educated ministry for the new country which they were helping to develop. As early as 1835 they began to agitate the need of a college centrally located in Michigan.

It should be recorded that the enterprise under way was not the first attempt by Free Baptists of Michigan to develop a trained ministry. In 1835 Rev. B. F. Nealy, the first missionary of the Free Baptist Home Mission Society to enter Michigan, opened a school in his log-cabin home at Howard. It was conducted successfully as Randalian Seminary during a period of four or five years. Rev. S. L. Julian, Miss Amy Lord, and Miss Alice Abbott joined Nealy in 1836.

At the Michigan Yearly Meeting held at the home of Ira A. Reynolds in Franklyn, Lenawee County, in June, 1844, a resolution, drawn up by Elder Laurens B. Potter, was adopted concerning the establishment on a permanent footing of a Free Baptist school, and Lewis J. Thompson, of Oakland County, Henry S. Limbocker and Roosevelt Davis, of Jackson County,

[3] *Free Baptist Cyclopædia*, p. 339.

were appointed as members of a committee to see
about it. A convention was called in midsummer
and a Board of Trustees elected. The first meeting
of the Board was held at Spring Arbor in October,
1844, at which time the name of the institution was
changed from Spring Arbor Seminary to Michigan
Central College. Daniel M. Graham, a promising
young man graduated at Oberlin, was elected president and the infant school opened December 4, 1844,
with Graham as the only member of the faculty and
five students in attendance (the enrolment rapidly
increasing during the year). Classes were held in
a small, story-and-a-half, wooden building, formerly
occupied as a store. Two college buildings were
commenced in 1845. Spring Arbor was a pleasant
country town, four miles south of the Michigan
Central Railroad and about eight miles southwest
of Jackson on the State Road to Jonesville. A daily
line of stages each way furnished means of transportation. (In 1855, in more commodious buildings
erected in Hillsdale on College Hill, a site selected
by Dr. Ransom Dunn and a committee of citizens,
the college began a career of usefulness that has per-
sisted to the present day, winning for itself an international reputation for initiative and high scholarship and at no time in its history refusing to admit
a person on account of race, creed, or sex.)

Among the laymen who heartily seconded the
pioneer preachers in their efforts to establish this
institution were: Hon. Daniel Dunakin, Eli T. Chase,
of Eckford; Thomas Dunton and Herman Cowles, of
Battle Creek; Joseph Blaisdell, of Assyria; Roose-

SARAH HARPER REYNOLDS

velt Davis, of Blackmer; Jonathan Videto, Joseph Bailey, and William Smith, of Spring Arbor.

Chauncey Reynolds, who had attended the Yearly Meeting in June and the special gathering later in the summer, gave personal endorsement to the proposals that resulted in the establishment of Michigan Central College (now Hillsdale). He was elected as a member of the first Board of Trustees and in this capacity served many years. His contribution to the newly-formed college of eighty acres of land was made on the condition that the gift should not be made available until the land would net $600 in materials or cash.[4]

In the summer of 1848 Edmund Burke Fairfield, pastor of the Free Baptist Church in Canterbury, New Hampshire, was called to the presidency of Michigan Central College. With Ransom Dunn, L. B. Potter and others, Fairfield was active in behalf of the college during those arduous and sometimes exciting days when the college was removed from Spring Arbor to Hillsdale. While at Hillsdale, Fairfield organized the North Reading church and was its pastor fourteen years.[5]

In 1852 Ransom Dunn, elected to the professorship of moral philosophy (in 1863 he became Burr professor of Christian Theology), began his long and devoted service as one of Michigan's pioneer builders. "During 1853 and the two following years he traveled with horse and carriage over ten thousand miles in the interest of Hillsdale College." [6]

[4] Hon. J. C. Patterson, in *Michigan Historical Collections,* Vol. VI.
[5] *Free Baptist Cyclopædia.*
[6] *Idem.*

He served two years as interim president of the college (1884-1886).

On July 4, 1853, the cornerstone of Hillsdale College was laid on the commanding summit of the hill that rises from the center of the city. The land that composed the college campus was the gift of Hon. E. Blackmar. In February, 1855, a new college law was enacted by the Michigan Legislature permitting Hillsdale College and all other State colleges to confer degrees. Under the law thirty-five trustees were elected in March, of which Ransom Dunn was one. Until his death, in 1900, he served as a member of this Board, attending thirty-eight out of the forty-three annual meetings.[7] His loyalty to the college is reflected in the academic record of members of the Dunn family. Of his eight children five were graduates from Hillsdale College and one (Cedelia A.) entered as freshman in 1858 and died during the year. Two children died in their early childhood. Nine grandchildren graduated from the college and three others attended as students. A great grandchild, Helen M. Gates, a nurse in India, was a student in Hillsdale College.

Doctor Dunn was often called upon by the ministers in the State to assist in evangelistic meetings. It was his privilege on one occasion to baptize twenty-five converts in Goble, Michigan, one of whom was a boy ten years of age named Harry S. Meyers, who later in life attended Hillsdale College and became the secretary of the United Society of

[7] *Life and Labors of Rev. Ransom Dunn, D. D.,* by Helen Dunn Gates, Boston, 1901.

RANSOM DUNN

the Free Baptist Young People and still later secretary of the Department of Visualization of the Board of Promotion and Finance of the Northern Baptist Convention, a position he holds at the present writing.

Dr. H. M. Ford has vivid memories of several of the founders of Hillsdale College and of Free Baptist churches in Michigan and gave the writer the following description of the personal characteristics of Fairfield and Dunn:

" It was a question whether Dunn or Fairfield was the greater preacher. They were so different they could hardly be compared. Dunn was chain lightning, a cyclone, a torrent, carrying all before him. His oratory at times was awe-inspiring, like standing before Niagara. Fairfield was like a modern four-hundred-ton locomotive sweeping majestically along without much noise and every part synchronized and working with absolute precision and drawing a half-mile load. His thought moved with majesty; he was the scholar, his presence and manner were impressive and held his listeners captive to the end. He was orator, preacher, poet, and actor all in one. He was a master in the use of Scripture phrase or the snatch of a hymn. Once I heard him quote these lines:

> " Princes, this clay must be your bed;
> In spite of all your towers,
> The tall, the wise, the reverend head
> Must lie as low as ours.

" It well-nigh threw me into a chill. As a political speaker he had no superior, and during the Civil

War he was constantly in demand, and also in the days of the Reconstruction. Doctor Dunn once said to me, ' I was always proud of him when on the platform.' "

The Sixth Annual Report of the Free Will Baptist Home Mission Society (1842), yields the following information concerning the early Free Baptist movement in Michigan:

" Previous to the time in which our missionary first entered the State of Michigan, which was in the autumn of 1835, there had been only one small Quarterly Meeting embracing some eight or ten churches, organized in the State. Since that time the Lord has wrought wonders in that new settled wilderness country. Although the labors of our missionaries in that State were principally confined to the Howard Quarterly Meeting, which was organized through their instrumentality, yet the Lord has blessed the labors of other faithful brethren who have gone into different parts of the State and have toiled and labored, enduring privations and hardships, subsisting on the scanty pittance which they carried with them, earned with their own hands, or received from the scattered new settlers of the country. Souls have been converted, churches have been multiplied, Quarterly, and even Yearly Meetings have been organized. Instead of one Quarterly Meeting which included all the Free Will Baptists in the State seven years ago, we now learn from the last official reports that in the State of Michigan, with a small portion of the northern part of Indiana, there are two Yearly Meetings, embracing eight

Quarterly Meetings, forty-eight churches, thirty ministers, ordained and licensed, and seven hundred and sixty communicants."

In 1856 there were seventy-two Free Baptist churches in Michigan, and in 1910, when the cooperation with Baptists began, there were 108.[8]

[8] Statistics furnished by Miss Helen E. Slayton, historian, College Church, Hillsdale, Michigan.

IX

FELLOWSHIP IN CHRISTIAN ACTION

Michigan Baptists do not forget their indebtedness to the New York Baptist State Convention which sent the first missionaries to the Michigan Territory. Note has been made of the pioneering work of that gospel explorer, Elon Galusha, who, in 1822, recognized and encouraged the young church at Pontiac, and was instrumental in planting the standard of the Cross at other points and whose initial efforts were carried on to fruitful harvests by Elkanah Comstock, the first ordained minister to locate as pastor of a Baptist church in a *white* settlement in Michigan.

I. THE FIRST MICHIGAN BAPTIST ASSOCIATION

Baptist churches in Michigan, from the days of the pioneer church in Pontiac to the present, have shared their pastors with needy outlying communities and in so doing are as truly missionary as the city, State, and national mission agencies that assist in the support of mission enterprises in this and other lands.

The first association of churches formed in Michigan was the Michigan Baptist Association (now the Detroit Association) that was organized in Pontiac in 1827. It was composed of four churches, all in Oakland County: Pontiac, with thirty-eight members; Stony Creek, with forty-six members; Troy, with forty-one members; and Farmington, with fourteen members. The first session of the association was held in Pontiac June 2 and 3, 1827. There were fourteen delegates present, with Mr. Comstock as the only ordained minister. One other ordained minister, Rev. Moses Clark, of Farmington, belonged to the association, but he was absent. Also in the association were Lemuel Taylor, of Stony Creek, and John White, of Troy, who had been licensed to preach. Lemuel Taylor had begun a ministry in Stony Creek before Comstock's arrival in the State. He preached the gospel not only in Stony Creek, but in the neighboring communities. The church at Stony Creek was the second Baptist church formed in the State.

An item in the minutes of this first session of the pioneering " Baptist Association of Michigan " attracts attention. The Association adjourned to meet at " Stony Creek on the first Wednesday in June, 1828, at ten o'clock a. m., Elder E. Comstock to preach the introductory sermon, Elder Henry Davis his substitute." The latter, a recent arrival in Michigan, was a young man of vision and strong faith from the Hamilton Theological Institution in New York who had begun a ministry in Detroit. He established in that growing community the First Baptist Church on October 20, 1827.

Mr. Albert H. Finn, in the *Baptist Centenary— Detroit, Michigan,* has defined for us vividly the spirit and purpose not only of an associational but of a city, State, or national fellowship of Baptists:

" In these days throughout our entire denominational life the association has surrendered its responsibilities largely to the State Conventions, or in the major cities to the City Unions.

" In the early days the association was the rallying point, the social factor, the missionary force among the churches. In Baptist polity the local church is always an independent entity, a law to itself, the one and only legislative body, but our Baptist work has never flourished where the spirit of cooperation has not gone hand in hand, so to speak, with the spirit of self-reliance and independence. Our association-wide, our State-wide, our nation-wide and our world-wide expression of a whole-hearted response to the Great Commission, is ever and always has been marked with a fine spirit of loyalty to our Christ, his imperative command, and our love for our fellow men. The Baptist denomination is the finest exemplification of democracy, both in the local church and also in our voluntary associations, in the larger tasks of the Kingdom. The love of Christ constrains, impels us—not obedience to man or man-made hierarchy.

" Thus it was that the Michigan Baptist Association, from the very first, evidenced its interest in the neighboring settlements where the gospel was not yet preached. Over roads and under conditions that nowadays, I fear, would deter the best of us, the ministers and laymen pushed out in helpful service to bring the gospel message to those who otherwise would not hear it. Many of those old heroes of the faith I can well remember, as our home was always an open house to those valiant souls who counted not their own lives dear that Christ might be preached. Men like Father Cornelius, Supply Chase, A. E. Mather, John Donnelly, Philo Forbes, Alfred Owen, S. Haskell, A. M. Swain, T. S. Wooden, N. C. Mallory, F. B. Cressy, Z. Grennel and others."

II. MICHIGAN BAPTIST STATE CONVENTION

The Michigan Baptist State Convention was organized in the First Baptist Church of Detroit, August 31–September 1, 1836.[1] Delegates from twenty-eight churches were present, although the records state that there were fifty-two Baptist churches in Michigan with 2,000 members. Among the delegates was Orisson Allen, of Pontiac, " Michigan's original Baptist."

The Convention from the first has stood for education and world-wide missionary effort. When incorporated February 16, 1842, Section 1, of Article III in the By-laws, read (and so stands today) :

" The purpose of this corporation shall be: To promote in the State of Michigan the preaching of the Gospel, Ministerial and General Education, the establishment, maintenance and assistance of Baptist churches and Bible schools, and the care of worthy pastors, their wives or widows, and their dependent children.

" To give expression to the opinions of its constituency upon moral, religious and denominational

[1] Ref., " Historical Statement," by Rev. George H. Waid, Recording Secretary, in *Michigan Baptist Annual*, 1935.

matters, to promote denominational unity and efficiency in effort for the evangelization of the Northern Baptist Convention, and by affiliation with that Convention to promote its plans and work."

From the first a major emphasis was placed upon education. Commending the efforts made to establish the Literary Institute at Kalamazoo, the Convention appointed a committee to study and devise means of establishing such a college.

Loyalty to the National Societies has been a tradition in the Michigan Baptist Convention. Grateful to the Home Mission Society for its pioneer work in establishing Baptist churches in Michigan and for the aid rendered to the Convention in its missionary efforts the Convention has ever given to this Society and the Woman's American Baptist Home Mission Society an equitable place in its programs and offerings. Likewise with the Foreign Mission Societies and the Publication Society relations have always been amicable and actively helpful.

Rapid growth of Baptists in the early years was due to the increase in population and the earnest evangelism by devoted missionaries. In 1894 the high water-mark in number of baptisms was achieved, 4,635. During 1935 the number of baptisms totaled 3,044 and the membership of convention churches reached 60,060.

III. Bible Schools Fostered from an Early Day

Michigan Baptists early in their history recognized the importance of the Bible school as an integral part of church life. A State Sunday School Commission was formed in 1869 to cooperate with The American Baptist Publication Society. In 1871 the Michigan Baptist Sunday School Association was organized and the following year reported 224 schools with a membership of 2,154.[2] In 1874 the work of the Association was brought under the supervision of the Convention. From an early day until the present time the Publication Society has constantly lent its aid to the State in the " promotion of the cause of Christ by improving the character of our Sunday schools; by developing and educating teachers and workers; by aiding feeble churches to sustain themselves by means of the Sunday school work and to plant and foster Sunday schools in destitute but promising fields." The Society has sent into the State colporter-missionaries and has cooperated in the support of State directors of religious education.

IV. PIONEERING FOR LIBERAL EDUCATIONAL POLICIES

The right to confer degrees by Michigan denominational colleges was secured under a general college law of 1855. Prior to this time the Legislature had granted private charters to two colleges only, giving them the degree-giving power. Michigan Central College (later Hillsdale), of Spring Arbor, and St. Mark's College, of Grand Rapids, were the two fortunate schools. In 1851 two women received the B. S. degree and in 1853 one woman the A. B.

[2] John E. Smith in *Baptist Centenary—Detroit, Michigan,* 1926.

degree from Michigan Central College. These were the first full academic degrees awarded to women by a Michigan college. In 1853 Michigan Central College closed its doors with the intention of moving to Hillsdale.

"It soon became evident that a new charter would be necessary to enable the institution (Michigan Central College) to make the desired move and it was seen that this could be secured only by a concerted effort. Other denominational schools had been founded and were also anxious to obtain collegiate rank. . . There was but one way out: a general law permitting the corporation of colleges. . . The leaders for the denominational schools were Doctor Stone (President) of Kalamazoo, Dr. Asa Martin of Leoni, E. B. Fairfield (President) of Hillsdale, President Sinex of Albion, and Professor Hosford of Olivet, while President Tappan of the University and a number of skilled lawyers and politicians opposed the bill. They argued that it was infinitely wiser and more preferable to continue to confine the right to confer degrees to a single State-controlled University.

In the course of the struggle another issue was injected into the debate, creating no little furore. This was concerned with co-education. It was well-known that the denominational schools were far more liberal than the University in this matter. Until 1870 no women were admitted to the University, while all the denominational institutions had been, for all practical purposes, co-educational from the beginning, although the form of a separate female department was generally maintained. There were separate graduation exercises and a few classes which were exclusively for either one sex or the other, but in most cases the young men and the young women recited together. As we have stated, Michigan Central College had gone so far as to award regular literary degrees to women. Doctor and Mrs. Stone (of Kalamazoo) were both strong believers in co-education, but, probably because of the force of public opinion, they had maintained the fiction of separate departments and had given women graduates only " Ladies' Diplomas." At any rate the advocates of women's rights became ardent supporters of the cause of the denominational schools when the University raised the bugaboo of granting degrees to women. The issue was accepted and the right defended by the friends of the small colleges.

After heated debates in both Senate and House a general college law was passed, and approved by the Governor on February 9, 1855. The first institution to be chartered under the act was Kalamazoo College. Hillsdale was granted a charter the same year. Michigan Union College in 1857 (changed to Adrian in 1859), Olivet in 1859, Albion in 1861, Hope in 1866, and Alma in 1887. In each case the right to confer degrees was granted with the proviso that the work done be as thorough as that required by the University.[3]

V. MICHIGAN BAPTISTS OPPOSE SLAVERY

Michigan Baptists were at the forefront of the antislavery movement. President E. B. Fairfield of Hillsdale College, as a Michigan State Senator in 1856, made one of the strongest addresses of the period against slavery. President and Mrs. A. B. Stone of Kalamazoo " advocated abolition for years and had preached it to their students." [4]

One of the most positive statements regarding the attitude of Michigan Baptists toward Negro slavery

[3] Goodsell and Dunbar in " Centennial History of Kalamazoo College."
[4] *Ibid.*

in the United States is found in the Seventh Annual Report of the Free Will Baptist Anti-Slavery Society. The clerk of the Van Buren Quarterly Meeting wrote in 1853:

I have a somewhat thorough knowledge of the feeling and action of our brethren in this (Van Buren) Quarterly Meeting; and I rejoice in being able to say that it is generally understood and almost universally acknowledged among ourselves, and those around us, that Free Will Baptists are uncompromisingly and unflinchingly opposed to American slavery and that this opposition is maintained at the ballot-box. I hesitate not to say that a large majority of the voters, connected with this Quarterly Meeting are bold to vote against slavery. Every minister among us licensed or ordained, regards it as a part of his business to preach against it, and then to vote as he preaches. There are some churches in the Quarterly Meeting of whom it would be safe to say that every voter votes against slavery. Two of our churches are situated in towns which gave a majority vote last fall against it, and Free Will Baptists have done at least their share to bring about this result. Still some vote with one or the other of the old political parties, at times at least. I devoutly pray that Free Will Baptists may avail themselves of this opportunity to remove the stigma cast upon them by the author of the book referred to in your communication.

From information received from other parts of the State, we are authorized to say that the above is a fair representation of our cause in the other Quarterly Meetings. The slave has no more true and earnest friends than in our ministry and membership in Michigan.

VI. The First Colporter-Missionary Wagon

Since the days of John the Baptist the emissaries of Christ have sought a hearing for the gospel in

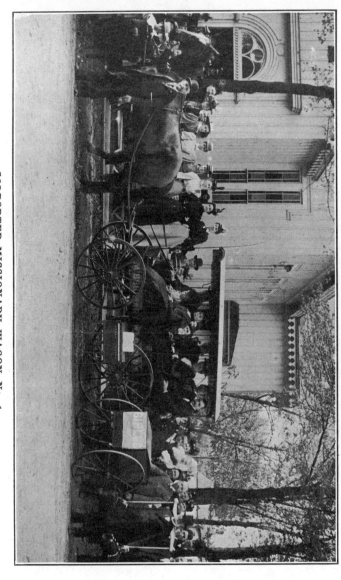

COLPORTER - MISSIONARY WAGON No. 1

Dedicated at Plainwell, Michigan, May, 1897

Rev. E. M. Stephenson, Colporter, holding team

remote, neglected places. For many years Northern Baptists have supported colporter-missionaries who at first traveled on foot, patiently and prayerfully, to carry the gospel message from house to house and from individual to individual. In recent years these missionaries have been sent out under the joint commission of The American Baptist Publication Society and The American Baptist Home Mission Society, and their itineraries are supervised by the State Convention within whose boundaries they labor. The term " colporter " is formed by the combination of two Latin words, *collum*, the neck, and *portare*, to carry, so that a colporter is one who carries his Bibles and religious books and tracts in some kind of bag or case suspended by means of a strap thrown about the neck.

The first wagon used by a Baptist colporter was built and dedicated in Michigan. We are indebted to Mrs. M. E. D. Trowbridge for the details concerning its inception and equipment.[5]

" The desire for such a wagon came to Rev. E. M. Stephenson, after some bitter experiences with heavy hand-bags, long walks, and many other unpleasant situations. The first move was the writing of a letter to Rev. John Fletcher, of Plainwell; one to Aunt Lizzie Aitken, Chicago; and one to Dr. R. G. Seymour, Philadelphia; all of whom agreed that the idea was good and hoped for success. Letters were then sent to all Sunday schools south of the Pere Marquette Railroad. During the winter an amount

[5] *The History of Michigan Baptists* (1909). Used by permission.

sufficient came in to purchase a team and harness, and Mrs. Fletcher, of Plainwell, gave the wagon.

" In April, 1897, the outfit was dedicated at Plainwell with appropriate exercises, participated in by the leading members of the State Sunday school Board and President Slocum, of Kalamazoo College. The first year's work was a surprise to the most enthusiastic and the report placed this kind of missionary enterprise on a permanent footing. The experiences of the summer, however, made it clear that a wagon better equipped for camping out was necessary; hence the original wagon and first team were sold at a profit and the money deposited in aid of a model wagon and better team. A little more money was raised, and in April, 1898, at Jackson, where the wagon was built, and where a State Sunday-school Convention was called for the purpose, the new wagon and team were set apart for service, Rev. J. Fletcher delivering the sermon and Doctor Seymour making the missionary address.

" The first fifty weeks of service with the new wagon resulted in the following:

" 3,863 miles traveled; 301 meetings held; 434 sermons and addresses; 2,082 families visited; 499 Bibles and 590 Testaments sold; 151 Bibles and 161 Testaments given; 1,008 books sold and 918 given; 73,795 pages of tracts and 225,565 pages of religious papers distributed.

" Wagon No. 1 was followed by No. 2, sent to Utah in charge of Jay Pruden, of Michigan. No. 3, built in Grand Rapids, was dedicated in the spring of 1898."

Fellowship in Christian Action

The colporter-missionary is in every way a pioneer, and like the frontiersman with whom he labors, he is willing and able to carve out and win a place for himself in desert places, forests or mountain wildernesses. All he asks is that we discharge in like spirit our reasonable responsibility for his support. He has responded to the challenge of a difficult yet worthy task. Shall we do less?

The colporter-missionary has a real hope and program. He is full of courage, resourceful, and like a prospector, he rejoices in his task and believes in his opportunity. Every day he is thrown into contact with men and women who are willing to deny themselves many of the comforts of life for the sake of developing the material resources of the country, and in like manner he foregoes and undergoes much for the development of the religious life of the country in which he has chosen to work.

"Should I not be willing to pioneer for souls?" Unequivocally the missionary answers this question in the affirmative.

The long journeys in heat or cold are unavoidable, yet he accepts them philosophically as something to be borne without complaint. It is not so difficult to endure hardships that cannot be escaped when at the end of a long drive a comfortable home and an appetizing meal await him. But not infrequently he is his own housekeeper and is obliged to cook his own meals and even the homes that are hospitably opened to him are apt to be destitute of many of the comforts common to more-settled communities. Yet he never feels that he is uncared for.

Nor are the people in the isolated homes he enters made to feel any sense of shame because they have nothing better to offer him, for a missionary can adapt himself to frontier hardships. He is never patronizing, whether the meal is a sumptuous one or of the simplest possible kind. With him whatever is offered is always a feast.

"Yes, this is my parish," said one of these missionaries. "Every day it reveals unlooked-for beauties. It is never the same. I love it and do not wish to be elsewhere. While I miss the inspiration of a city parish, where the stimulus of a large audience is an advantage, yet here I have a compensation which the city pastors have not. The eagerness of the people in these remote communities to hear the gospel is something beautiful to see. Everywhere I find a welcome. Yes, I love it here." [6]

VII. BAPTIST BEGINNINGS IN DETROIT

Baptist work in Detroit was begun in 1827 by Henry Davis, a young man from the Hamilton Theological Institution. It has been recorded that Mr. Davis was sent to Michigan by the Baptist Missionary Convention of New York. This is a true statement. Davis was the missionary of the New York Convention, but in this connection it should be noted that the Baptist Missionary Society of Massachusetts also contributed to his support. An account of the activities of Mr. Davis was given at the twenty-

[6] This description of the nature of the work of the colporter is from *Old Trails and New*, by Coe Hayne. The Judson Press, Philadelphia.

fifth anniversary of that beneficent organization, on May 28, 1828, prior to which time an appropriation of one hundred dollars had been made by this Society for Mr. Davis for one year in Michigan.

Henry Davis arrived in Detroit, July 2, 1827, and entered on the duties of his vocation with great earnestness. In a letter to the Massachusetts Society he wrote:

" Our assemblies were rather small at first, although sufficiently large to afford us some encouragement. By visiting and becoming better acquainted with the citizens, our congregation was regularly increased. At present (October, 1827) we have an assembly which will bear a good comparison with those of other denominations. Baptists were never known in Detroit until we commenced our meeting. Consequently we could not expect to find a people prepared for us. Since my arrival I have had the pleasure of baptizing three persons. There are now twelve, including myself and wife, who have regular letters of dismission. We have called a council to meet on the 20th of October with a view of organizing a church. To effect this object we have to send two hundred and fifty miles down the Lake (to the New York Convention) for ministering brethren."

The secretary of the Massachusetts Society adds: " The Society will lament to hear that this devoted servant of Jesus is at present, if not altogether, laid aside from public usefulness. After mentioning that he had started from Detroit, with a view of procuring funds for a house of worship, he was taken sick, from which illness he has not recovered. He writes:

" 'I cannot express to the Board the feelings which have exercised my mind, on account of being obliged to relinquish the important and promising station at Detroit. Already had the Lord enabled me to collect a small but promising church. I had baptized five persons. We had obtained an influence in Detroit far beyond our expectation. We had also obtained a donation from the Corporation at Detroit, of a valuable lot for the erection of a meeting-house. We had formed a very promising Sabbath school. In the Territory of Michigan, I prevailed on the brethren to form a promising Tract Society; and had formed another in Upper Canada. The field was just opening and smiling in prospect, when the Lord saw fit to deprive me of health, and thus oblige me to leave it. But he knows what is best. His will be done. I cannot close without urging the Board to continue its patronage to the little church at Detroit.' "

The departure of Henry Davis from Detroit was not the end either of the man or his work. In 1909 Mrs. M. E. D. Trowbridge, in her *History of Baptists in Michigan*, published this statement by " the late Rev. W. W. Everts, D. D.": " The first pastor and one of the founders of the First Baptist Church (in Detroit) was the late Dr. Henry Davis. He helped me to procure an education and was a life-long and inspiring friend."

Henry Davis devoted his life to good advantage if he helped W. W. Everts to get an education. For twenty years Doctor Everts was pastor of the First Baptist Church of Chicago. Due chiefly to the contribution of this church while he was pastor of it, the (old) Chicago University and Theological Seminary were founded and their buildings erected. He rebuilt the Walnut Street Church in Louisville, Kentucky, in 1852, at a cost of $40,000 and cleared the Bergen Heights Church, New Jersey, of an indebtedness of $35,000. He was the author of the *Pastor's Hand-Book* and other books and tracts, and for many years was one of the most prominent ministers of Christ in the United States.

Detroit Baptists are glad to date their organized church life back to the coming of Henry Davis. The infant church that Henry Davis founded struggled valiantly for life during several years. In October, 1834, Robert Turnbull, of Connecticut, became the pastor of the church and the first missionary of the Home Mission Society to settle in Detroit. From one of his letters we learn that in November, 1834, the population of Detroit was 5,000, of whom 800 were French, 800 Irish, and about 200 Dutch and Swiss. There were a thousand unnaturalized foreigners. The remaining portion were from all parts of the United States. Thus at this early date Detroit was cosmopolitan. The Baptists, who were completing their new meeting-house ("a beautiful, brick building, good size, well-proportioned and delightfully situated"), numbered about forty and had nearly one hundred in the worship service before the new building was available. There was a Sunday school of forty children with seven teachers.

Ebenezer Loomis, one of the most striking figures among Michigan's pioneer ministers, was one of the speakers at the dedication of this first Baptist meeting-house in Detroit, January 11, 1835. His journeys throughout the Territory as the "exploring agent" of the Home Mission Society were performed on foot. His fame as the "walking preacher" extended beyond the borders of the Michigan Territory, yet his reason for adopting that exclusive mode of travel was simple: "My journeyings have been performed on foot," he wrote in 1833. "I have in many places gone where I could not have traveled with a horse, and in many instances could not have found keeping for a horse. In one or two instances I have felt the need of one, in crossing rivers, but on the whole concluded that walking is the best. My health has been good, for which and numberless other mercies, I have cause for gratitude to God."

VIII. DETROIT BAPTIST UNION

Today—one hundred and nineteen years after the arrival of the youthful theological student from Hamilton—Detroit Baptist churches occupy a conspicuous place in the Protestant fellowship of Detroit and Wayne County. The progress that these churches made during one hundred years has been graphically recorded in their anniversary volume published by The Michigan-Detroit Baptist Association Centenary Committee (Albert H. Finn, Secretary and Editor) and to this publication the writer is indebted for much of the data appearing in subsequent paragraphs of this chapter.

The Michigan Association (now the Detroit Association) was organized in 1827 as the first feeble attempt of the Baptists in the State to associate together for mutual helpfulness and inspiration. Out of this fellowship grew the Detroit Baptist Union, a standard city mission society that has had a long history of missionary achievement in a city that during the past third of a century has grown with amazing rapidity. The first record of this organization appeared in the *Detroit Free Press* of May 7, 1878, on which date a mass-meeting of Baptists was held in the First Baptist Church, at which a nominating committee was appointed. Dr. W. W. Everts, of Chicago, who, in his youth was helped by Henry Davis, Detroit's first Baptist minister, gave the principal address. On May 20 the committee reported a list of officers that included, Doctor Gleiss reminds us, "A German, a Frenchman and a Negro." [7]

While the Detroit Baptist Union has generously supported during their formative periods many struggling churches composed of people of the older American stock, from an early day it has taken a position of undisputed leadership in work in behalf of New Americans and Negroes. Sensing the need because of the rapid expansion of Detroit, the Union has led in endeavors involving tremendous sacrifices in order that unchurched neighborhoods in many parts of the city might have religious

[7] H. C. Gleiss, *History of the Detroit Baptist Union,* 1926.

privileges. In 1917 the present general superintendent, Dr. H. C. Gleiss, assumed executive direction
of the work of the Union. With him have been associated consecrated home missionaries, both men and
women, and together they have led in one of the
most versatile and extensive city mission programs
within the territory of the Northern Baptist Convention. In 1920, in cooperation with the Publication Society, the Department of Religious Education
was created. Two directors of religious education
have ably served the Baptists of Detroit—Rev.
Arthur V. Allen and Rev. Ben T. Leonard.

IX. THE FIRST B. Y. P. U. OF A. CONVENTION

The first convention of the B. Y. P. U. of A. was
held in Detroit. The year was 1892. With 4,100
delegates in attendance, it was a memorable occasion. Mr. Earl J. Batty, president of the Michigan
State B. Y. P. U. in 1926, in his paper " Our Baptist
Young People," contributed to the centenary volume
of Detroit Baptists, said:

"An item of particular importance is, that this
gathering was the first general convention which
had been held since 1845, at which were present
representatives from the territory of the Southern
Baptist Convention and the Northern Baptist Convention. In addition, there were the Canadian Baptists. The Convention remains indelibly impressed
upon the minds of those who attended as one of the
greatest experiences of their lives. Here in Detroit,
Albert H. Finn was one of the most active workers.

He was president of the City Union (was largely instrumental in its formation), a member of the Board of Managers of the B. Y. P. U. of A. and also on its Executive Committee."

Under date of November 30, 1935, Mr. Finn wrote:

" The B. Y. P. U. was organized to serve all Baptist causes and organizations, John H. Chapman, a Chicago business man, and Dr. L. Wilkins, an Iowa pastor, being the outstanding leaders in the movement.

"At the Detroit Convention there were delegates from Maine to California and almost every intervening State and Territory, the Southland and four provinces of Canada, England, China, and India. The speakers on the program were representative ministers and laymen from the nation at large and Canada, not forgetting Doctor Clough home on furlough. The convention was epoch-making in its messages and far-reaching in its progressiveness and its challenges. Most heart-stirring was that feature known as the ' Salutation of the Flags.' Many of the States already had organized into State B. Y. P. U.'s. Each State so organized—twenty-three responded—had its own flag. The representatives marched to the platform to the strains of ' Onward, Christian Soldiers.' Dr. J. Lansing Burrows, of Georgia, secretary of the Southern Baptist Convention, and one of the speakers on the Convention program, arose and said that he had come from a State that had not as yet organized and so he was left out but he wanted to be taken in the procession, and if he could not get on the band-wagon he would fall into line in the rear. As he had no banner he would like to march under ' this banner,' and he raised the Stars and Stripes. The applause was tremendous. Doctor Fulton suggested that Doctor Burrows, accompanied by a lady carrying the national colors, ascend the platform. The compliance with the suggestion created an enthusiasm indescribable.

"Among the brethren from the Southern Baptist Convention, in addition to Doctor Burrows, were Dr. J. B. Cranfill, of Texas; Dr. J. B. Gambrill, of Mississippi; Dr. George B. Eager, of Kentucky; Dr. L. L. Henson, of Maryland; Doctor Early, of Tennessee; Doctor Penrod, of Arkansas; and Doctor Wranch, of Virginia."

X. THE ROGER WILLIAMS GUILD

Over thirty-four years ago Baptists in Ann Arbor became convinced that a special Christian ministry should be afforded the Baptist students in the University. Rev. Thomas W. Young, pastor in Ann Arbor (1894-1906), was the leader in the movement. The Michigan State Convention in 1902 endorsed his plan. The Baptist Students' Guild (now the Roger Williams Guild), was organized and a building secured. By the generosity of Mr. A. Q. Tucker the mortgage on the Guild Hall was paid and the Hall dedicated in 1906 as the " Tucker Memorial Hall." The first Guild director was Allan Hoben (September 15, 1904). He was soon called to the pastorate of First Church, Detroit, and was succeeded by

Fellowship in Christian Action

Warren P. Behan (February, 1905). Five others followed: Fred Merrifield, John G. York, Newton C. Fetter, A. Wakefield Slaten and Howard R. Chapman. The latter entered the work on September 15, 1919, and is now completing his seventeenth year as university pastor, a notable record. The activities of these men have followed three broad paths according to Mrs. Helen Beman in *History of Ann Arbor Baptist Church:* "(1) Making friendly and helpful contacts with students. (2) Acting as advisor for students in their religious and social activities. (3) Giving systematic religious instruction through classes." Hundreds of students, having gone out from under the influence of these men, are now exerting a beneficent influence in church and denomination. Six of the more recent graduates are in the active Baptist ministry; another, Miss Sigrid Johnson, is a missionary nurse in India. Support of the Guild is shared by the Michigan Baptist Convention and the Board of Education of the Northern Baptist Convention. It maintains a strong Deputation Team, consisting of men and women. They serve in various helpful ways large churches as well as small.

XI. ROYAL AMBASSADORS

The Royal Ambassadors of Michigan, affiliated with the national missionary organization for boys of that name, have maintained a camp for five years. It is located at Lake Copneconic, near Fenton. Last summer (1935) eighty-seven boys were in attendance. There were thirteen pastors and laymen on the faculty, affording the boys a well-rounded religious, social and recreational program. The director of the camp from its inception has been Rev. W. T. Huxford, of Kalamazoo. Rev. E. A. Kelford, of Eaton Rapids, is the dean.

X

MICHIGAN WOMEN ORGANIZE

I. WOMAN'S BAPTIST HOME MISSION SOCIETY OF MICHIGAN

The *Christian Herald,* of April 9, 1873, published a statement showing the need for Baptist women to organize for home mission service. This statement invited all who were interested to attend a meeting in Detroit on April 29, 1873, and was signed by fifty women. As a result of this conference the Women's Board of Baptist Missions was organized, but three years later the name was changed to the Woman's Baptist Home Mission Society of Michigan, under which name it was incorporated in 1891. The primary object of the organization was to promote missionary work in the State, but soon Michigan women were contributing to general home mission work in North America.

Within the State, especially around the lumber camps and mines large groups of immigrants had settled. These people included Poles, Italians, Danes, Swedes, and Germans. Some counties were without a Baptist church, and where churches did exist the membership was often too small and poor to support a pastor. The State Mission Board had begun work with the pioneer churches and the immigrants, but gladly welcomed the cooperation of the women. Besides assisting in the work of the State and the programs of The American Baptist Home Mission Society, Michigan women, in 1893, began contributing to the Women's Baptist Home Mission Society with headquarters in Chicago. During the first thirty-three years of its history the Michigan Society received and disbursed $105,456.57.

According to the Thirty-third Annual Report, published October 16, 1906, Michigan churches had 294 women's Mission Circles besides Young Ladies' Societies, Junior Mission Bands, and Baby Bands. The work was fully organized in twenty associations, and was reported regularly to headquarters.

In 1909, by unanimous vote, the Michigan Society decided to become a part of the national organization, the Woman's American Baptist Home Mission Society, an account of the formation of which is given in a booklet entitled *Together,* published by this Society in 1933 and from which the above account of the Michigan organization was taken.

II. WOMAN'S BAPTIST FOREIGN MISSION SOCIETY OF MICHIGAN

BY MRS. MARY COOPER LEETE, of Detroit [1]

Our Society does not claim to have started Foreign Mission work among Michigan women. That was done as early as 1871, when the women of our land, moved like Mary of Bethany to bring a special love-gift to their Saviour, organized Women's Circles in many of our churches for missionary work.

[1] From *History of Baptists in Michigan,* Detroit, 1909.

Michigan Women Organize

These mission circles were to supplement the work of our general societies by sending out women missionaries to work for the women and children in heathen homes and to teach in mission schools. The officers who had this work in charge for the Central and Western States were in Chicago, and the organization was called the Society of the West. A State Secretary was appointed for each State, and this Secretary acted as a magnet to hold together the separate circles. Dr. Caroline H. Daniells first held this position in Michigan, and Mrs. Sophia Bronson Titterington and Mrs. Harriet Swegles followed in turn. These were the pioneer workers in the State, and so well did they work, and so responsive were the women, that in 1878 there were 131 circles contributing about $2,000 a year to foreign missions; and, best of all, four Michigan women heard the call, "Who will go?" and answered, "Here am I, send me." These were Miss Mary Rankin, Miss Helen Watson, Miss Anna Sweet, and Dr. Caroline H. Daniells. But there was no State organization of these workers, and so no recognized place in our State Convention, and none of the inspiration which comes from union in service.

The time had come for this step. Doctor Daniells went as our first medical missionary to China in 1878, and her going and her letters home wonderfully quickened missionary enthusiasm. The State Convention met at Kalamazoo in October, 1879, and the women interested in foreign missions met too, and, adopting a State Constitution, organized as a State society auxiliary to the Society of the West.

As Minerva sprang from the head of Jove, full grown and fully armed, so this society seemed full grown and armed for service at that inaugural meeting. Officers were elected, and a State expense fund was determined upon, the State was to be kept informed of the work through a column in the *Christian Herald;* the Society of the West was invited to hold its next annual meeting in Detroit; Mrs. Bronson and Mrs. Clough, returned missionaries, gave inspiring addresses. Doctor Daniells sent an appeal for a hospital in Swatow, China, and the genuineness of the enthusiasm was proved by the fact that, in a few moments, $500 was raised for that purpose; the mother of Doctor Daniells giving the first $100. Is it any wonder that after such a meeting the State Convention passed a resolution that " The Woman's Baptist Foreign Mission Society of Michigan be an acknowledged part of the State Convention "?

III. MICHIGAN BAPTIST WOMEN UNITE [2]

BY MISS FLORENCE E. GRANT

Ex-President The Woman's Baptist Mission Society of Michigan

In 1909 the two national societies which had been organized in the interests of Home Missions, Woman's Baptist Home Mission Society with headquarters in Chicago and Woman's American Baptist Home Mission Society with headquarters in Boston, decided to combine in one organization and invited the Michigan society, which, although contributing

[2] From *Baptist Centenary—Detroit, Michigan,* 1926.

to the work of the two societies, had maintained its independence during these years, to join with them. After much deliberation, because the contributions to work in the State, which had been very dear to the hearts of these women since their organization in 1873, would have to be withdrawn, it was decided to unite with the newly organized society. The State organization was continued as heretofore with the same officers and same plans of work, but all contributions were sent direct to the Woman's American Baptist Home Mission Society with headquarters in Chicago.

As the year went on it was found that the two women's organizations in the State were overlapping in their work and that the same results could be accomplished by one society, so in 1913 steps were taken to unite the two societies and in 1914 the Woman's Baptist Mission Society of Michigan was organized. This society was incorporated under the laws of the State of Michigan, November 3, 1914. This society is auxiliary to the Woman's American Baptist Foreign Mission Society and the Woman's American Baptist Home Mission Society and carries out in the State the plans made by the two national societies. The circles in each association in the State have formed an organization which meets at the time of the annual association meeting and has officers and secretary-directors corresponding with those of the State society. . .

The national societies have been entertained in the State on many different occasions, the most important of these being the meeting of the Society of the

East and the Society of the West for the purpose of consolidation under the name of the Woman's American Baptist Foreign Mission Society. This was in 1914. At that time the District plan was adopted and Michigan became a part of Central District.

IV. ONE IN SPIRIT AND SERVICE

BY MRS. W. H. DORRANCE
President Woman's Baptist Mission Society of Michigan

When the Woman's Baptist Foreign Mission Society of Michigan united with the Woman's American Baptist Foreign Mission Society we had in legacies about $2,300, and this was turned over to the Detroit Baptist Union for the purchase of the Italian church, formerly the Berean Mission of the Woodward Avenue Church.

If I were to declare what had been the outstanding accomplishment of the past six or seven years (1929-1936) I would say it was in the very decided spirit of cooperation that has animated our members and the workers in the whole State Convention. There is a correlation of all our interests that is largely due to the efforts of our State Executive Secretary, and his recognition of the value and importance of the woman's department of service. Our deputation work is carried on almost exclusively through the State office and the workers there aid us greatly in office detail. We are one in spirit and service. This is evidenced in one way by the Executive Secretary furnishing transportation for the representatives of the Woman's Society to all the mid-

year meetings and giving them full time on the
programs. In return for this the various heads of
the woman's work strive to secure a large attendance
at these meetings. In many other ways the work is
cooperative. Mr. Andem often attends our Board
meetings and his suggestions are welcomed ever.

Another phase of work that has proved mark-
edly successful has been our Guild and Woman's
House Parties; the Guild will celebrate its Tenth
Anniversary House Party this next year and the
women their sixth. The attendance last year exceeded three hundred in the woman's party. The
programs are inspirational and educational and a
spirit of Christian fellowship is ever in evidence. In
addition to the State House Party several associations have echo parties of their own of from one to
three days; these are within the reach of many
women who could not attend the State affair.

The women have from one to three students at the
Baptist Missionary Training School in Chicago each
year either receiving State scholarships or associational. It has proved to be money well invested.

A budget of seven hundred dollars is allowed for
our work each year, but three hundred dollars of
this amount is paid to Miss Frances Priest as our
Christian Americanization missionary. Her work
in the State is supported cooperatively, the Woman's
American Baptist Home Mission Society assuming
a share of her salary.

Miss Eunice Monroe, who received our scholarship at the Baptist Missionary Training School in
Chicago, is now in Alaska at the Kodiak Orphanage

as a representative of the Woman's American Baptist Home Mission Society—a direct contribution from the women of the State.

V. WOMEN'S WORK IN MICHIGAN DURING THE PAST TEN YEARS

BY MRS. GEORGE WREGGIT

Recording Secretary Woman's Baptist Mission Society of Michigan

1926 and 1927

The women of Michigan worked very hard and faithfully, raising funds for the Mary Trowbridge Dormitory of the Kalamazoo College. As far as can be ascertained from the minutes, $5,275.82 was raised. President Hoben announced November 4, 1926, as the date set for the opening of the Dormitory, an invitation being sent out to all women's organizations in the State to attend the opening. Much time and effort was spent in putting the " Golden Jubilee Fund " across. The records show Michigan raised $23,528 as her part in this drive.

Another outstanding event of 1927 was the first World Wide Guild House Party. This was held in the Mary Trowbridge Dormitory at Kalamazoo in July and has become an annual affair and very helpful in the Guild work. During the year a Civic Secretary was added to the Board and this work has been developed in the State.

1928

While the minutes record nothing outstanding, they do show that the women were working, organizing new Guilds and Children's World Crusade Bands, promoting the woman's work through the State.

1929

Cooperated with the State Convention more definitely than ever before. Convention increased the budget for the woman's work.

1930

The outstanding event of this year was the Woman's House Party at Kalamazoo. This has become an annual event. We have outgrown the accommodations at Kalamazoo and this year we accepted an invitation to have our summer program at Hillsdale. This program included the two house parties and the summer assembly of our young people and Sunday school workers. We had 301 registrations for the Woman's House Party, taxing the accommodations at Hillsdale; so this year we are to try a new plan and have two sessions for the women, each session to be for three and one-half days.

1931 and 1932

During the years that the woman's work has been organized in Michigan the women have raised funds for scholarships at the Baptist Training School in Chicago. This has been a real worth-while effort when we receive reports of the splendid work being done by some of these girls who have received their appointments, as they are telling the old, yet ever new story " Of Jesus and His Love."

In 1931 the Prayer Leader Secretary was added to the Board and has worked hard (as strange as it may seem for those interested in the Master's work) and faithfully to find prayer leaders for each association and each church.

1933

We cooperated with the Convention program and featured the Sixtieth Anniversary of the Woman's Baptist Home Mission Society of Michigan and Free Baptist Woman's Mission Society of Michigan, this Convention being held at Kalamazoo. In this year something entirely new in the Christian Americanization work was carried out in the Saginaw Valley Association. The program covered a whole month— April 17 to May 17. This program was carried on in all the churches in the association, including training classes conducted by Miss Frances Priest, also pastors' training classes conducted by Mrs. E. H. Kinney and Dr. Ralph Taylor Andem. This plan has been carried on in several of the States since.

1934 and 1935

In 1934 an intensive program on Christian Friendliness was put on in Detroit by Miss Priest and the pastors.

We are cooperating this year with the State Convention in the plans being made for the Centennial.

VI. WORLD WIDE GUILD—ANCHORED IN PRAYER

Helen Crissman was born on a farm near Mt. Vernon, Michigan. Her parents were Charles Elmer

Crissman and Margaret Rust Crissman. Her father was the superintendent of the Mt. Vernon Baptist Sunday school. Among her earliest and most vivid recollections is an experience that came to her when she was five years old. She was at prayer-meeting with her father where only six or seven persons were present. Kneeling beside her father, she heard Mrs. Elsie Farmer pray that someone from that little country church would go out into Christian work, and she felt and still feels that she was the answer to that prayer.

At twelve Helen Crissman joined the Mt. Vernon Baptist Church and was baptized by Rev. Will N. Ferris. (This church was sold and torn down in 1921. The church-bell was moved and is now in a new church in East Lansing, Michigan.)

Helen's education was begun in the " Crissman " district school. She went six miles to the Romeo High School, graduating in 1909. She attended Kalamazoo College, where she found the whole atmosphere Christian and missionary. Many graduates, home on furlough, came to speak in chapel. In later years she declared that she tried to appear indifferent to these messages, but could not forget the words of that prayer in the Mt. Vernon country church. A close friend was Edith Olsen, whose sister Esther was in Africa. Edith planned to devote her life to Christian work until she was taken ill, the doctor pronouncing the trouble tuberculosis and recommending that she go to Colorado at once.

" Helen, I wish you would work in my place," said Edith when she left.

The next year Helen Crissman was offered the Michigan scholarship in the Chicago Baptist Training School, and upon her graduation from that institution was appointed by the Woman's American Baptist Home Mission Society to work among young women, seeking to interest them in definite service and special training. At about this time the World Wide Guild was launched to become the missionary organization of Baptist girls. Miss Crissman was appointed by the Women's Mission Societies as the first national field secretary of the Guild. At the beginning of her work she wrote to Edith, who was still fighting tuberculosis in Colorado Springs, and told her that she had not forgotten her request. She promised Edith that she would try to do double duty if Edith would be her prayer partner. Thereafter Helen always sent Edith her schedule of speaking engagements. Taking into account the difference in time Edith planned to be in prayer at the very time the other was attending a conference or public service. Often Edith would write to girls who had special problems or who were considering definite Christian service.

The consistent growth of the Guild and the results of its work are known. Starting under the Women's Boards and carried on later by the Department of Missionary Education of the Board of Education, it has served the churches in a distinctive way as have the chapters of the Royal Ambassadors, the missionary organization for boys. Miss Crissman organized a chapter of the Guild in Casper, Wyoming, and there met an earnest young minister to whom she was married in 1922. But her Guild work was not ended. During that first year as a pastor's wife in Wyoming she was asked to visit the Michigan and Indiana Assemblies. During Rev. Calvin Thompson's nine years' pastorate in Barbourville, Kentucky, she made frequent trips back to Indiana and Ohio for associational and State rallies. Then in September, 1932, the two began their work in the Delaware Street Baptist Church in Syracuse, New York. Almost immediately Mrs. Thompson was appointed World Wide Guild District Secretary of New York. Her very first field work was done in New York State and now she was back in the State, and again doing Guild work. She declares that she gets a real thrill as she goes out over the State for associational rallies to find in existence star chapters that she had organized in the early days of Guild history. In several instances she has found daughters of star-chapter Guild girls carrying on in their mothers' places. Her chief work as District Guild secretary has been the District Guild House Party, meeting for a week on the campus of Keuka College. During the summer of 1935 there were 372 girls registered there.

And now this interesting word from a pioneer Guild organizer to the Guild girls of every land:

" Edith from her bed in Colorado Springs was the secret of the spiritual power of the Guild in its beginnings," said Mrs. Helen Crissman Thompson in a recent letter. " She lived for six years as my prayer partner. The little poem which she sent to me expresses the spirit of our work together. (I

K [133]

do not think the poem is original with her except in certain lines) :

> " Now send in my place, O Master,
>   Some one I dearly love
> To the people who sit in darkness
>   With a message from above.
> I have learned my own unfitness
>   For the task I vainly sought;
> But others are ready and willing,
>   And the work will yet be wrought.

> " But since in the grand fulfilment
>   I still would have a share,
> Choose one in my place, O Master,
>   Whom on my heart I bear.
> Her work, and her aspirations,
>   Her hopes, my own shall be;
> And around by the way of Heaven,
>   I shall reach each W. W. G.

> " And if we labor together,
>   Says one of the chosen band,
> We shall reap and rejoice together—
>   Oh, the joy of that other land!
> If I must be one of the number,
>   Whose *strength* is *just to lie still*,
> Dear Lord—through my beloved—
>   Teach *me* to *do thy will*.

" I have one little daughter, Helen Ruth, two and a half years old. She just came to the door and asked: ' Mother, are you working? '

" This brings the story up to date and I can answer: Yes, I'm still working in home and church and I'm still a Guild secretary, and as much interested as ever.

Michigan Women Organize

" Across the fields of yesterday
  There often comes to me,
A little girl with face aglow,
  The girl I used to be.
She listens, watches, takes my hand,
  And walks awhile with me,
And asks me if I've made myself,
  The woman I'd planned to be."

XI

MISSIONARY OUTREACH OF MICHIGAN
BAPTISTS

Of the hosts of forward-looking boys and girls who have gone out from humble homes to accept hard tasks in obscure corners of the earth, Michigan has contributed and is contributing her large share. To the foreign fields have gone at least one hundred and thirty-seven young people from Michigan homes, churches, and colleges to serve as preachers, teachers, doctors, and missionaries' wives.[1] How many more have accepted calls to difficult urban and rural fields in the homeland, it is difficult to answer. In our reckoning it would be unjust to omit the names of men and women who have served in struggling churches that have not received help from mission boards, either State or national. Yet it is impossible for the writer to present this shining roster. A partial list of home missionaries who went out from Michigan homes, schools, or churches is given in the *Appendix*. It is possible to make reference here only to a few individuals who by their Christian devotion have enriched other lives and other communities in foreign lands and in America. Others have labored as faithfully and their ministries have blessed a needy world.

[1] See list of names in Appendix.

Missionary Outreach of Michigan Baptists

John Scott

On a farm near the village of Northville, twenty miles west of Detroit, lived George Scott and his wife, Abigail Hart Scott. To them four sons and one daughter were born, of whom John was the eldest. In the country school of the district the boy gave evidence of a genuine love for study and his parents, with a vision that was the common heritage of many of the pioneer home-builders, decided that he should go to college. In commenting on this a brother in later years said: " John it was who first saw beyond the fences of the old farm and broke over the family traditions, went to college, and for the time being became an alien. When he returned at the end of the first year, the younger members of the family began to have enlarged visions as a result of his initiative."

Entering Kalamazoo College in the autumn of 1866 he remained there two years; in 1871 he graduated from the University of Rochester with high honors.

Through the influence of this country boy other boys of the neighborhood were led to seek higher educational advantages than the little district school afforded.

After his graduation from the Rochester Theological Seminary in 1874, John Scott began the active life work for which he had been long dreaming and preparing. Pastorates in Ohio, Michigan, and Minnesota were followed by a brief period of illness. Upon recovery and true to his ideals, he again looked for an opportunity to enter Christian work. For a time he was employed in Chicago as the business manager of *The Young People's Union,* the official organ of the B. Y. P. U. of A., and then came to him a call from The American Baptist Home Mission Society to become a teacher in its mission schools. First at Shaw University, Raleigh, North Carolina, as professor of theology and later as president of Bacone College, Muskogee, Oklahoma, he made the great contribution of his life in teaching and inspiring youth of two underprivileged racial groups, Negro and the American Indian. Impartial critics, viewing the period of nearly ten years spent by President Scott in devoted service in behalf of Indian boys and girls, declare it to be a memorable one in the history of the school. Under his kindly Christian guidance he built character, he instilled high ideals, brought men and women of different races into wholesome fellowship, for he had both red men and whites in his classes. President B. D. Weeks, the present head of the school, told the writer that he often meets Doctor Scott's pupils throughout the Southwest and elsewhere who bear enthusiastic witness to the helpful influence of the man and the soundness of his educational methods.

Of Doctor Scott, his beloved teacher, former Secretary of War, Patrick J. Hurley, wrote:

"President Scott was my most unselfish friend. He gave me the opportunity that has made possible what little success I have enjoyed. He had no selfish motive in giving me the opportunity to secure an education. His mission in Indian Territory was to convert and educate the Indians. I was not an Indian. He was a Baptist minister. I was of another faith. He was drawn to me by no ties of blood. He didn't even know my relatives. He never saw me until the day he asked me to go to his school. His interest in me was purely because of his desire to help one who needed help. What he did for me he did for thousands of others. Today I stand with uncovered head in reverent recognition of the wonderful services he rendered me and the powerful and wholesome influence he has had upon my life. I thank God that I knew him."

The other three boys born to George and Abigail Scott were Zar D. Scott, for many years a prominent Baptist layman in Duluth and engaged there in the lumber business; Arthur P. Scott, who was a farmer and died at Northville, Michigan, some years ago; and George K. Scott, who is still living and is engaged in raising cotton in the Imperial Valley of California. All three boys grew into men of sterling character and were a credit to their family and to the community in which they lived. Zar D. Scott was particularly interested in religious matters, and being a man of some means was a consistent contributor to our missionary enterprises, especially foreign missions.

LIDA SCOTT ASHMORE

Another member of the family of George and Abigail Scott was a daughter, Lida, who left this

Michigan countryside in her youth to seek an education and find useful employment in behalf of needy people. Eventually she entered missionary service in distant China. As the wife and unfailing lieutenant of Dr. William Ashmore, Jr., her contribution to the success of the Swatow Mission was a notable one. She began her work there in January, 1880, and left the mission with Doctor Ashmore in November, 1926. Her death occurred but recently; her husband, now retired from active service, survives her.

Mrs. Lida Scott Ashmore's first and most important work, according to her testimony, was the caring for her husband, "making it possible for him to do his work," and the instruction of two children. The two William Ashmores, father and son, gave one hundred years of service to China. One of the abiding contributions of William Ashmore, Jr., to the South China Mission was the translation of the Bible into the Swatow colloquial. The work was completed December 3, 1920.

Before her marriage to William Ashmore, Jr., Mrs. Ashmore had sailed to Burma as the wife of Rev. Albert J. Lyon, to start a new mission among the Kachins of Upper Burma. Mr. Lyon was a man of unusual promise, struck down early in his career as a missionary by a tropical disease. His untimely death, only a few weeks after their arrival at their destination, left her a widow, and she returned to the United States, where she did a most useful work in speaking to the churches.

In Swatow she had charge of the Girls' Boarding

School from 1882 to 1898. Deeply interested in the education of the Chinese girls, she started day-schools for girls at a number of the inland churches. To finance these schools she started the making of drawn work by Chinese women and girls, and she was so successful that from her earnings she was able, not only to provide for the day-schools, but also to put up, and turn over to the Board, free of cost, a greatly needed new building for the Girls' Boarding-School in the compound, which was named after her mother, The Abigail Hart Memorial School.

During her first furlough in the United States she was asked to contribute a series of mission studies to *The Ensign*, a Baptist weekly published in Minneapolis, a service that she rendered most acceptably.

Toward the close of her life on the mission field, in connection with the celebration of the Sixtieth Anniversary of the South China Mission, she prepared a vividly written and most interesting " Historical Sketch " of the mission from its beginning up to that time, the year 1920.

For years she served on the Building and Property Committee of the Mission, much of the time as its secretary. At the meetings of the committee, her suggestions were always most helpful in problems not always easy to solve.

When her husband was Mission treasurer she was assistant treasurer, and took care of the work during his absence in the country. At one time he was asked by the Home treasurer to meet in Hong Kong and forward on their way to Burma and India a party of missionaries who were coming across the Pacific. Mr. Ashmore was not able to get away, so she took his place, and put the business through under trying circumstances. It was the time of the World War, and all sorts of restrictions and un-looked-for situations were encountered. But she was equal to the occasion and surmounted all difficulties, and got the last member of the party aboard the steamer in time for the sailing.

During the World War she was in charge of a section of the Red Cross work, and was awarded a decoration for efficiency in that service.

Energy, courage, tact, kindness, helpfulness, resourcefulness, all were characteristic of Mrs. Ashmore, and she left a host of friends among the Chinese and foreigners who knew her, and who still cherish her memory and speak of her with affection.

JOB H. SCOTT

Reared in the same neighborhood where lived his cousins, John and Lida Scott, was another youth, Job H. Scott, who joined that long procession of Michigan's sons and daughters who set their faces toward the far horizons and never retreated when the going became difficult. For thirty-two years he was a member of the Japan Mission. When he was retired from active duty in 1924 he had given two years of service beyond the age of seventy, and with Mrs. Scott was returning home by way of India and Europe when he died in Port Said, January 12, 1925.

The devoted couple had expected to spend a year with a son, Prof. Harold Scott, of Robert College, Constantinople.

Simple, impressive memorial services were held, first, in Japanese, at the Naniwa Baptist Church in Osaka that the missionary had served so long, then, in English, in the Osaka Union Church. Both Japanese and foreigners called attention to his love and loyalty, patience and faithfulness.

CAROLINE H. DANIELLS

From the heart of a girl born in Troy, Oakland County, Michigan, sprang a desire that in later life blossomed and bore abundant fruit. Caroline H. Daniells at the age of fifteen responded to a call to devote her life in service as a foreign missionary. Keeping ever warm this resolve, she spent four years at Olivet and Oberlin Colleges, graduating from the latter institution in 1867. She was a teacher for a time, and then in 1871 the Woman's Foreign Mission Society of the West was organized and she was asked to become State Secretary for Michigan. But not for an hour did she relinquish the thought that some day she would be in a foreign land working for the under-privileged in the name of her Master. Completing a medical course in Cleveland, she accepted an appointment as the first woman medical missionary in South China. She was the first medical missionary to be appointed by the Woman's Foreign Mission Society in the West. She was Michigan's gift to the Orient.

Baptist Trail-Makers in Michigan

From 1879 until near the close of her work in China, Miss Daniells carried on a spirited correspondence with Dr. J. N. Murdock, corresponding secretary of the Foreign Mission Society. The excerpts the writer selected from their letters on file in the rooms of the society should be of particular interest to Michigan people.

Miss Daniells to Doctor Murdock, October 4, 1879:

You will have learned before this reaches you that I have asked a grant from the Society of the West. I did it after having looked the ground carefully over and I have faith that " In His own way the Lord will provide."

Doctor Murdock to Miss Daniells, December 12, 1879:

Could you have witnessed as I did the prompt response of the ladies of Michigan to your call for aid in establishing a hospital; seen how readily, nay enthusiastically they contributed the first $500 toward it, I am sure you would have been gratified. . .

Doctor Murdock wrote the above at a time when Baptists everywhere were not whole-heartedly in sympathy with a missionary policy of expansion that included the establishment of dispensaries, infirmaries, and hospitals as a real part of the work of evangelization.

" I recognize them not only as humane but even as Christian agencies," he continued in his letter to Miss Daniells under the above date, " but they must be mainly the outgrowth in the people themselves; the most you can do is to give them a miniature pattern of institutions which have sprung up in the

wake of Christianity as it has advanced among the
nations. So much I think we ought to do, and we
must do it as soon as we can. Let your patience
have its perfect work. . .

"I had the pleasure of meeting your mother in
Kalamazoo (place of Convention), and you have
seemed a little more real to me ever since. Her heart
is with you, with a true motherly tenderness and
pride, but if possible more with your noble work.
The Lord comfort her abundantly for all she has
given up, and give her all she has desired." (This
mother pledged the first $100.—AUTHOR.)

Miss Daniells to Doctor Murdock, February 4,
1880:

I am with good heart asking God daily to open the way
for me . . . to give me a hospital if He sees best, and above
all to grant me patience to do His work in a spirit that shall
honor His Cause. . . My patience shall have its perfect work
and while I wait the opening of one channel, I will do my
best in what is already open to me. I am glad you have
visited Michigan and added so much to the interest of the
meetings of the Convention which I have always thought
inspiring. I wish you might know more of my mother than
a single meeting could give you."

Miss Daniells wrote in 1881:

Foreign mission work is certainly not of men, else it would
have ceased long ago. I often feel that my life could be
better spent than doing a work which is so little prized by the
very people to whom I have come. But this is only momen-
tary; for the presence of the Master comes about me, and
I seem to hear, "Not for these, but for me, have you done
it." And I go on with comfort in the thought.

And in 1883:

My work has become very dear to me. The horrors of heathenism, which impressed me so painfully at the outset, are eclipsed by the gospel as I see it applied to these who already believe; and I am very grateful that I am allowed to work in a line that is so acceptable to a very needy class of women. I have a Bible-woman who finds good opportunity, and does good work in the hospital, besides two others whom I am training as nurses.

To *Our Medical Work in the Orient,* a publication of the Foreign Mission Societies, we are indebted for the following graphic account of the work of Michigan's pioneer woman medical missionary:

Our medical work in this most needy country was begun in South China in 1879, when Dr. Caroline H. Daniells, a graduate from the Medical Department of Wooster University, Cleveland, began her work in the treaty port of Swatow, on our mission compound at Kakchieh, across the bay from the city proper. Great need of medical work indeed did she find on her arrival for, although there was a fine Presbyterian hospital across the bay in the city of Swatow, there had never been a woman doctor and the women and girls on our side of the bay were numerous and much in need of medical care. Thousands of Chinese villages had not even heard of the splendid work done by the Presbyterian hospital. In one case when a man with gangrene of the foot applied to the surgeon of that hospital for medical help and was told the foot must be amputated, he replied that he must first consult his native doctor. The native doctor, characteristic of his class, exclaimed in wrath: " That foreign devil says it must be amputated, does he? Well, I can amputate, too," whereupon he had the suffering patient place his leg across a log and with a rusty axe cut off the foot. The man of course died.

Missionary Outreach of Michigan Baptists

When our first medical missionary began her work in the Swatow district, we had no hospital or dispensary building, and she had to travel among the hundreds of villages, where great crowds sought her aid. At times she would have fifty decayed teeth to be pulled in one brief stay of a few hours. Hundreds of blind children—blind perhaps as the result of worms—were brought by parents begging piteously that they be given sight.

Doctor Daniells was obliged to begin medical practice at once. Soliciting funds from her Society (Woman's Foreign Mission Society of the West), she had a small building erected which could accommodate twenty women, meanwhile studying the workings of Doctor Gault's hospital and maturing plans for establishing one for women.

Our first woman doctor in China worked hard and well and though her health began to fail when she had been but a short time on the field, she continued bravely, preparing prescriptions to be carried by others when she could not go herself. When her lameness prevented her from doing actual work, she spent her time Romanizing a handbook of medical terms in the Swatow dialect or writing letters to interest people at home in the work. So the work went on making progress each year in spite of difficulty until finally Doctor Daniells was compelled to return to America.

As Doctor Daniells was never able to return to the field our medical work in Swatow was suspended for five years, until in 1889 the Society succeeded in finding a woman to fill the vacant place—Dr. Anna K. Scott, who for the following twenty-five years did such a masterful piece of work in the South China district.

FRIEDA A. DRESSEL

Thirty-nine years ago Miss Frieda A. Dressel went to Utah, under appointment by the Woman's American Baptist Home Mission Society, as a missionary among the Mormons, " with," she said in a recent letter, "the call of God to the work in my heart and enthusiasm tingling to my finger tips."

Miss Dressel was born in Ganges, Michigan, of German parents who had come to this country early in life. They belonged to the state church of their native country, but when they settled in Ganges began at once to attend the Baptist church there, although they never united with it. It was into this church that Miss Dressel was baptized. She was educated in Michigan, being graduated from the Fenton Normal School and later took a commercial course in Chicago. There had always been a great desire in her heart to do mission work, but there seemed no way open for her to secure special training. At last the Immanuel Baptist Church of Chicago, of which she was then a member, sent her as its representative to the Baptist Missionary Training School of the same city. On her graduation she went to work in Provo, Utah, and in Utah she has remained to this day.

The contribution Miss Dressel has made in that land of uncertainties may be gaged best by one who has lived in Utah to hear the testimonies of people who have shared with her the difficulties of carrying on in Christ's name in Mormon territory. She is one of Michigan's best gifts to the Far West.

JAY PRUDEN

One of the most persevering and efficient colporters under the commission of the Publication Society was a native of Michigan, Jay Pruden, to whom reference already has been made.

" He was born near St. John, in October, 1867," related Mrs. M. E. D. Trowbridge.[2] " One season he walked regularly nine miles to school. He was converted and baptized in 1890, studied in Kalamazoo College, and for a time was pastor at Burr Oak. During the summer of 1892 he walked thirteen miles on Sundays, caring for three Sunday schools and a young people's meeting. Illustrative of his patience and perseverance, he visited one schoolhouse, six miles away, five Sundays in succession when no one came; but at length a good Sunday school was established. In December, 1892, he was commissioned by the Publication Society as colporter. Ill health led him to change climate, and he went to Utah in 1897, engaging in the same work. In February, 1900, he returned to Michigan to act as Sunday-school Missionary, in which service he was eminently successful. In the interest of health he again sought change of climate and in 1907 removed to California.

" One evening after a weary day's work, Colporter Pruden found himself in a violent snow-storm, carrying in his hands two bags containing books and Bibles. He did not know where he was going to rest for the night. While looking for a lodging through the blinding snow he heard a voice calling him: ' Stranger, don't you want to come in out of the storm? ' He discovered a humble home in which there was an old man and his aged wife. He went in and accepted their hospitality, and endeavored to

[2] *History of Baptists in Michigan,* 1909. Used by permission.

talk with them on the subject of religion before re-
tiring; but his message was received almost with
curses, and he retired to rest with a heavy heart.

" In the morning the old gentleman and his wife
met him as he was coming out of his sleeping apart-
ment and said: 'Stranger, have you a Bible?' He
said: 'Yes, but why do you ask such a question after
last night's declarations?' The old man replied:
'We want you to read it to us and pray with us.'
Then the colporter said: 'I would like to know why
you changed?' The old man said: 'Stranger, do
you know you talk in your sleep?' He replied,
'No.' 'Well, wife and I have been kept awake by
hearing you say every little while in your sleep,
"Oh! that they might know Jesus;" and we want
to know Him.'

" This man and his wife were converted; and a
few weeks later they drove seven miles to a Baptist
church in order to make their confession of faith."

CLAUDE H. BARLOW

Michigan made a large contribution to the cause
of world brotherhood when Claude H. Barlow (born
in Lyons, Michigan, in a Baptist parsonage) entered
China as a medical missionary under appointment
by the American Baptist Foreign Mission Society.
We are indebted to Dr. James H. Franklin, president
(1935-1936) of the Northern Baptist Convention,
for some of the details in the story of his eventful,
useful life. [3]

[3] *Missionary Review of the World*, November, 1925. Adapted by
permission.

In 1912 Doctor Barlow was obliged to return to America to enter a sanitarium to be treated for pulmonary tuberculosis caused by his effort to save a patient in his mission hospital at Huchow in East China. A Chinese patient, ill with tuberculosis, requiring surgical attention for some minor trouble, was brought to the hospital. Although Doctor Barlow used the utmost care, the patient ceased to breathe as soon as the anesthetic was administered. As the hospital was not equipped with a pulmotor, Doctor Barlow placed his own lips against those of his patient and succeeded in reviving him. As a consequence of his heroic act the young physician the next year was at Saranac Lake ill with pulmonary tuberculosis.

Upon his recovery Doctor Barlow came to Doctor Franklin's office at the Foreign Mission Rooms in New York City and asked to be sent back to China. He was reminded that China with its wretched sanitary conditions was no fit place for a man recovering from tuberculosis.

"I am fit."

To prove his assertion Doctor Barlow peeled off his coat and struck his chest with his fists. The gesture was a convincing one.

So back to China went Doctor Barlow in 1914. On his way there he stopped in England for a few months' post-graduate study at the London School of Tropical Medicine.

In 1921 a letter came to the Foreign Mission Society from Johns Hopkins University which read in part:

" One of your missionaries, Dr. C. H. Barlow, of Shaohing, China, is here with us for a few weeks. We find that he has been making a study of the life history of a certain fluke which in the form of intestinal parasites is discovered in the bodies of many Chinese and often proves fatal. He has had no proper laboratory facilities in China, but if your Society will release him from the regular missionary work for twelve months and allow him to continue his study of the fluke, we will find money to provide a small building and necessary equipment at Shaohing."

Of course the Foreign Mission Society would release a worker for such a Christian service, and at Doctor Franklin's office, a few weeks later, arrived Doctor Barlow with his suitcases crammed with bottles and jars and with a story that Doctor Franklin reported as follows:

" Several thousand Chinese in a single province were afflicted with a disease that, to the layman, looked much like dropsy. After two or three years, they died unless something could be done to free them of the intestinal parasites. To cure the individual was not difficult if he could be brought to the hospital for proper treatment, but the disease could not be controlled in that way. Several hundred thousand patients could not be cared for in the hospitals. The origin of the disease must be discovered. Some one must trace the parasite to the breeding-places; that is, discover the foodstuffs in which the germ appeared. But that required a properly equipped laboratory and there was none near Shaohing. If the doctor could take some of the full-grown flukes to America he could easily study them in a laboratory! But our immigration laws would not permit him to bring them here in the body of a sick Chinese."

But the flukes were brought to America.

"How did you get them over here?" Doctor Franklin asked the young scientist.

"Well," replied Doctor Barlow, "one Sunday morning when most of the assistants were at the church services, I took thirty-two of the flukes from the body of a patient in the hospital, put them in a tumbler, locked my office door and drank them down."

The memory of the experience seemed very vivid to the doctor, observed Doctor Franklin.

"Did you tell any of the other missionaries what you had done?" inquired Doctor Franklin.

"No," answered the other.

"Did you tell your wife?"

"No. I did not tell anyone. I boarded a ship and came to America."

Doctor Franklin continues the story.

"I do not know how long Doctor Barlow allowed the flukes to multiply in his own body, but after several months he presented himself at Johns Hopkins University and told his story to the amazed experts, who gladly helped him to free his body of the parasites and to make a careful study of them. One of the experts with whom I sat at table on a Pacific liner last year told me that only one of the flukes survived the treatment given them at Johns

Hopkins and that Doctor Barlow slept and ate in the laboratory watching it lest the temperature change suddenly and something go wrong with the experiment. He had only one chance. In April, 1922, I found him back in his little laboratory."

What ending can we give to this thrilling story? Doctor Barlow succeeded in tracing the parasite back to a species of land snail and advised the Chinese Government that if the snails could be destroyed the disease would disappear. Johns Hopkins University has printed the Barlow Monograph, which tells the remarkable story of the human intestinal fluke: *Fasciolopsis buski.*

"Nothing less than the spirit of the Eternal Christ could have prompted such a sacrificial service," declared Doctor Franklin. "It must compel Chinese and others to inquire, 'In whose name and by what power have you done this thing?'"

Under the sponsorship of the Rockefeller Foundation Doctor Barlow, during recent years, has been carrying on investigations in Egypt and the Sudan in an effort to find a way to kill off snails that are carriers for a parasite that is the source of the flat worm disease that afflicts between sixty-five and seventy per cent. of the Egyptian population. The persistent stalking of this parasite until the doctor had traced it to its breeding and feeding places forms a stirring chapter in modern scientific explorations. The *New York Times* of April 23, 1933, carried a long account of Doctor Barlow's four years in Egypt. In the Sudan Doctor Barlow conducted his experiments on King Fuad's estate.

Missionary Outreach of Michigan Baptists

XII

WHAT THE FUTURE HOLDS

I. " WE ARE THE PIONEERS OF THE NEW CENTURY "

BY RALPH TAYLOR ANDEM

Executive Secretary of the Michigan Baptist State Convention

God has placed before Michigan Baptists a challenging future, full of opportunity.

First, an opportunity to renew spiritual enthusiasm. Michigan Baptists must have the vital, fresh, contagious enthusiasm that comes from marveling at each new day's store of spiritual blessing as we consciously walk with the Lord. One hundred years old, yes! But childlike in faith, in a warm, spontaneous desire to tell what the Lord has done for us.

Secondly, an opportunity to increase. (a) *To increase in numbers.* During the last hundred years we have averaged a net yearly increase of six hundred—a net increase of one for every one hundred Baptists in Michigan. God calls mightily for a greater increase than that. Our evangelistic spirit, the attractiveness of our daily life is challenged! Let us go forward. (b) *To increase in giving.* We close the first hundred years giving for local expense at the rate of three cents per day per member, and for missions all over the world one-third of one cent per day per member. We marvel that God has blessed so much more abundantly than we have given. The future challenges each Baptist to an honest stewardship. (c) *To increase in service. At home.* One hundred rural communities waiting to be entered by some evangelical church. Suburban districts outgrowing church facilities. Cities needing carefully planned ministry to bilingual groups. *World wide.* The world calls to Michigan Baptists to share more unselfishly our many blessings. (d) *To increase in wisdom.* What a challenge the new century gives Michigan Baptists in the realm of education. At present the lowest in the list of major denominations in giving our youth higher education, the new century calls for an honest attempt to increase in wisdom, not forgetting that all wisdom must be warmed in the spiritual life of Jesus Christ.

Thirdly, an opportunity to give leadership. Baptists have a great, an unique message for the world. Michigan Baptists should renew their realization of this challenge. From Michigan in this new century should come some of the finest leaders. *Leaders in spiritual things.* Our churches must produce the great pastors of the century. *Leaders in world affairs.* Christian Baptist laymen, who think in world terms, statesmen instead of politicians, who hear the call to such leadership as truly as the prophet hears his call. *Leaders in finance.* The Baptists of Michigan should be producing, consecrated, Christian financial experts who consider it a great calling to finance the Kingdom. *Leaders in education.* Teachers, professors, so Christian that to sit in their classes is to be led unerringly to the Master. Leaders in education who will count it a life-work to give spiritual glory and vision to the commonplace, secular education.

Fourthly, an opportunity to give oneself. The early years of our first century as Michigan Baptists were made glorious by pioneer heroism, volunteer work even under real sacrifice, a personal enthusiasm and earnestness that knew nothing but conquest, a personal responsibility that waited not for paid leadership nor wished to avoid real problems.

What the future holds for Michigan Baptists depends somewhat upon our pastoral leadership (and we have a consecrated, hard-working group of pastors as we enter the new century). The continual prayer of our pastors is that they might be better pastors. But what the future holds for Michigan Baptists depends largely upon the self-giving of 62,000 individuals called Baptists—trustees who consider no trust greater than being Christian trustees; deacons and deaconesses challenged to give enthusiastic support to the spiritual program of the church; laymen who are continually conscious that they must be stewards of their time and that to witness for Christ is their greatest privilege; young people who are willing to stand alone, if need be, to maintain the high standards of the Christian life; men and women living so attractively, so sincerely, so wisely that others will want to follow the Master.

The new century can see Michigan Baptists entering a real land of promise. There are giants, both real and imaginary, in the land. There are walls around human hearts, more difficult to conquer than the walls of Jericho. There are mountains that stand in the way and to which we must cry, " Who art thou, O great mountain? Before the works of Michigan Baptists thou shalt become a plane." We are the pioneers of the new century. And the same Leader or Saviour—the one who said, " Be of good cheer, I have overcome the world," challenges us to go forward. If we keep the faith, the future can hold nothing but *victory*.

II. BEYOND THE NEARER HORIZONS

Down through the decades every great political, social, or economic upheaval has brought in its wake a missionary opportunity. The population movements westward gave birth to our work upon the frontier. Work among Negroes—missionary and educational—had its beginning before the close of the Civil War. The development of railway transportation necessitated a further increase in the missionary forces in the remote western areas. The vast industrial growth of the United States, bringing alien millions to our shores, also brought to our doors a staggering need and an inspiring opportunity—the evangelization of foreign-speaking people. The Spanish-American War had its spiritual aftermath on every isle beneath the Southern Cross. The World War precipitated a sudden exodus of black people from quiet Southern cotton fields and plantations to the roaring industrial infernos of the North, that has no parallel in the history of any race.

The demand for cheap labor in the Southwest and Middle West started another population avalanche— an interminable stream of Mexicans across the border. We saw city and rural situations become increasingly complex as restless, questing people sought to adjust themselves to strange conditions that had arisen overnight.

What of today? Are there not opportunities presented to the youth of the land to pioneer for Christ, matching the spirit of our pioneering fathers? Reread the challenge so clearly given by Secretary Andem in this chapter and addressed to Michigan's 62,000 Baptists.

True obedience requires us not alone to acknowledge our loyalty to Christ but to allow his loving spirit to govern us in all human relationships, including marriage, the disposition of time, talents and wealth, temperance, peace, interracial and international relations, and the improvement of industrial conditions.

Do we not believe that inherent in the church is the power to meet every God-given task?

We are in a period of far-reaching economic readjustment. In our extremity God may see his opportunity.

In 1837, when the nation was in the grip of one of the severest financial panics of its history, the Home Mission Society sent word to John Mason Peck that its treasury was at such low ebb that there were no funds for the struggling churches he had founded in the Mississippi Valley. Peck did not give up. The word surrender was not in his missionary vocabulary. He asked permission to visit the stronger churches of Illinois, Missouri, Indiana, and Kentucky in behalf of the weaker churches on the frontier and the funds he solicited saved the western mission.

Thus in courageous faith were born the independent State Conventions of the West, among which Michigan has taken a prominent place.

When account is taken of great physical and social areas within the nations where religious privileges are still inadequate, it is seen that the Christian enterprise in America has barely begun. In industrial, suburban and rural communities have arisen problems that call for an unprecedented mobilization of Christian forces, national and local. The greatest missionary task that confronts Christian America today is to make America Christian. The very life of our foreign mission enterprise hinges upon it.

Confident that the evangelization of America is indispensable to World Evangelism, let us hew out of the wilderness of our doubts and hesitations a new conception of the word *pioneer*. Opportunity is given to us, not for defeat but for victory; not for security and sterile fear but for brave and joyous struggle.

Baptist Trail-Makers in Michigan

XIII

HISTORY OF YOUR LOCAL CHURCH

A PROJECT

Hebrews 11: 17 to 12: 2

(Reference, *The Torch Bearers*, Course VIII, Part III,
The Judson Press, Philadelphia)

Delegate several members of your group to present during the class session, or before the entire church or Sunday school, a history of your local Baptist church.

In the above enterprise the older settlers may with profit be questioned. They may recall incidents in the earlier periods of the history of your community that local histories do not record.

Search for stories concerning the earliest Christian work (Baptist or otherwise) in your community. Consult your local library and historical society. County histories are useful.

Secure the cooperation of the church clerk in your researches. The church minutes will yield interesting items of history.

At the anniversary exercises of a small church near New York City, held recently, a dramatic skit was built around the early business transactions of the church. The conversation carried on by those who took part was adapted almost entirely from the

church records. Old-fashioned costumes were worn.
Old articles and photographs were placed on display.

Make the occasion a time when special attention
is paid by the younger members of the church to the
aged members. The latter bore the burdens for us
during the earlier years of their lives. They are
worthy of our admiration, love, and esteem.

A section of the program might be devoted to a
review of one hundred years of Baptist work in
Michigan. This, also, could be worked out dramati-
cally.

BIBLIOGRAPHY

Baptist Centenary—Detroit, Michigan, Detroit, 1926.

History of Baptists in Michigan, by M. E. D. Trowbridge, 1909.

History of Baptist Indian Missions, by Isaac McCoy, 1840.

History of the Baptist Missionary Convention of the State of New York, by John Peck and John Lawton, Utica, 1837.

Baptist Missionary Magazine, Boston, 1826-1830.

A Century of Missions in the Empire State, by C. W. Brooks. The American Baptist Publication Society, Philadelphia, 1900.

Comstock Genealogy. Descendants of William Comstock of New London, Connecticut. Edited by Cyrus B. Comstock. Knickerbocker Press, New York, 1907.

The Baptist Encyclopædia, Cathcart.

Michigan Historical Society's Collections.

Missions (magazine), New York.

Journal and Letters (MSS.) of Abel Bingham. The American Baptist Foreign Mission Society, New York.

Letters (MSS.) of Leonard Slater. The American Baptist Foreign Mission Society, New York.

Murdock (J. N.)—Daniells (Caroline H.) Correspondence. The American Baptist Foreign Mission Society, New York.

Documents and Magazine Files. The American Baptist Home Mission Society, New York.

Autobiography of Laurens B. Potter. *The Advance*, Hillsdale, Mich., 1886.

Vanguard of the Caravans, by Coe Hayne. The Judson Press, Philadelphia, 1931.

APPENDIX

FOREIGN MISSIONARIES

Foreign missionaries from Michigan homes, churches, and colleges. (For additional names see page 171.)

Data compiled for this volume by Miss Jessie K. Bates of the American Baptist Foreign Mission Society.

(Names starred are those of missionaries appointed by the Woman's American Baptist Foreign Mission Society.)

	Born in Michigan	Sent Out from Michigan	Mem. of Michigan Church	Attended Michigan Schools
Ackley, Ernest L. _____	Yes	No	No	No
*Ambrose, Miss Emma O. _____	Yes	Yes	?	Yes
*Appel, Miss Frieda _____	No	No	Yes	No
Ashmore, Mrs. Wm., Jr. (Lida Scott, First husband A. J. Lyon) _____	Yes	Yes	?	?
*Bacon, Miss Edyth A., M. D. _____	Yes	No	No	No
Bahrs, J. Ross _____	No	Yes	Yes	No
Bahrs, Mrs. J. Ross (Mauriene Johnson) _____	No	Yes	Yes	No
Barlow, C. Heman, M. D. _____	Yes	Yes	No	Yes
*Barnard, Miss Mary Elsie _____	Yes	No	No	No
*Barnes, Miss Emily E. _____	No	Yes	Yes	Yes
*Bendelow, Miss Kittie E. _____	Yes	Yes	Yes	Yes
*Benjamin, Miss Lena A., M. D. _____	No	No	No	Yes
*Brewer, Miss Bessie M. _____	Yes	No	No	No
*Bromley, Miss Julia C. _____	Yes	?	No	No
*Buckner, Miss Olive E. _____	Yes	Yes	Yes	Yes
Burkholder, Mrs. T. W. (Julia Phillips) _____	No	No	No	Yes
*Carman, Miss Charity _____	Yes	No	No	No
Carman, Newton H. _____	Yes	No	No	No
*Cody, Miss Jennie L. _____	No	No	No	Yes
Coldren, Mrs. M. J. (Emma L. Smith) _____	Yes	Yes	No	Yes
Collett, Charles A. _____	No	Yes	No	Yes
Collett, Mrs. Charles A. (Dora Jenkins) _____	No	Yes	No	Yes
Collett, Charles P. _____	No	No	No	Yes
Collett, Mrs. Charles P. (Amy Mills) _____	No	No	No	Yes
*Corbin, Miss Helen L. (m. J. R. Goddard) _____	Yes	No	No	?
*Crane, Miss Florence N. _____	No	Yes	Yes	Yes
Crocker, Lionel J. _____	Yes	Yes	Yes	Yes
*Cronkite, Miss Ethel M. _____	Yes	Yes	Yes	Yes
Crozier, Galen G., M. D. _____	Yes	Yes	Yes	Yes
Crozier, Mrs. Galen G. (Mabel Bosworth) _____	No	Yes	Yes	Yes

	Born in Michigan	Sent Out from Michigan	Mem. of Michigan Church	Attended Michigan Schools
Curtis, Philip S.	Yes	No	No	No
*Daniells, Miss C. H., M. D.	Yes	Yes	?	?
*Daniels, Miss Ruth	Yes	Yes	Yes	Yes
Dickason, Frederick G.	No	Yes	No	No
Dickason, Mrs. F. G. (Bertha Bates)	Yes	Yes	Yes	Yes
Dowd, Willard F.	Yes	Yes	Yes	Yes
Dowd, Mrs. W. F. (Muriel A. Massey)	Yes	Yes	Yes	Yes
*Elgie, Miss Helen (m. J. H. Scott)	No	Yes	Yes	Yes
Finch, James A.	Yes	Yes	No	?
Finlay, George E.	No	?	No	Yes
*Finney, Miss Nona G.	No	No	No	Yes
Fisher, Royal H.	No	No	No	Yes
Ford, Fred B.	Yes	No	No	No
Forshee, Archibald A.	Yes	Yes	No	Yes
Fox, Url M.	Yes	Yes	Yes	Yes
*Gaylord, Miss Ella M.	No	?	Yes	No
*Gerow, Miss Katherine, M. D.	No	Yes	Yes	Yes
*Gifford, Miss Martha J., M. D.	No	No	No	Yes
Grant, James S., M. D.	No	Yes	No	Yes
Grant, Mrs. J. S. (Annie Shand)	No	Yes	No	?
Griffin, Mrs. Z. F. (Libbie Cilley)	Yes	No	Yes	Yes
Harper, Robert, M. D.	No	Yes	Yes	Yes
Harper, Mrs. Robert (Nellie Briggs)	Yes	Yes	?	?
*Hay, Miss Elizabeth E.	No	No	No	Yes
Hendershot, Clarence	Yes	Yes	Yes	Yes
Holtom, Daniel C.	Yes	Yes	Yes	Yes
Holtom, Mrs. D. C. (Mary Price)	No	No	No	Yes
Huizinga, Gerritt J.	No	Yes	Yes	Yes
Huizinga, Mrs. G. J. (Katie Telder)	Yes	Yes	Yes	No
Huizinga, Henry	Yes	Yes	?	Yes
Huizinga, Mrs. Henry (Susan Antvelink)	Yes	Yes	?	?
*Johnson, Miss Sigrid	Yes	Yes	Yes	Yes
Jones, Mrs. E. H. (Grace Van Valkenburg)	No	Yes	Yes	?
Kelley, Edwin D.	No	Yes	Yes	Yes
Kennan, Albert L., M. D.	No	Yes	Yes	Yes
Kennan, Mrs. A. L. (Phylana Ranney)	No	Yes	Yes	Yes
King, Judson C., M. D.	No	No	No	Yes
King, Mrs. J. C. (Cora Wolff)	Yes	Yes	Yes	Yes
Knowlton, Mrs. M. J. (Lucy St. John)	No	Yes	Yes	Yes
Kurtz, Frank	No	Yes	Yes	Yes
Kurtz, Mrs. Frank (Elizabeth Fletcher)	Yes	Yes	Yes	Yes
Latimer, Mrs. James V. (Jessie Adams)	Yes	No	No	No
Lougher, Edwin H.	?	Yes	Yes	Yes
Lougher, Mrs. Edwin H. (Minnie Whitney)	?	Yes	?	?
Malcolm, Fullerton B., M. D.	No	Yes	Yes	Yes
Martin, John Clough	No	No	Yes	Yes
Martin, Lewis E.	Yes	Yes	Yes	Yes
Martin, Mrs. Lewis E. (Nellora Clough)	No	Yes	?	No
*Martin, Miss Muriel (m. Dwight O. Smith)	No	No	Yes	Yes
Mather, Mrs. Asher K. (Ruth Delzell)	Yes	Yes	Yes	Yes
*Mather, Miss Ruth	Yes	No	No	No
Maxfield, Charles L.	Yes	No	?	Yes
Maxfield, Mrs. Charles L. (Florence Teachout)	Yes	No	?	?
*McCulloch, Miss Gertrude F.	No	Yes	Yes	Yes
*Mills, Miss Grace	No	Yes	No	No

Appendix

	Born in Michigan	Sent Out from Michigan	Mem. of Michigan Church	Attended Michigan Schools
Miner, Samuel E.	No	Yes	No	Yes
Moncrieff, Mrs. Jesse E. (Virginia Merriam)	No	Yes	Yes	Yes
Murphy, Howard R., M. D.	No	No	No	Yes
Murphy, Mrs. Howard R. (Emma Gehman)	No	No	No	Yes
Newman, Henry Ware, M. D.	No	No	No	Yes
Owen, Mrs. William C. (Elizabeth H. Pratt)	Yes	No	No	No
*Palmer, Miss Frances E.	Yes	Yes	Yes	Yes
*Parker, Miss Emily A.	Yes	Yes	?	?
*Phillips, Miss Sara G.	Yes	No	No	No
Proctor, Mrs. John T. (Nellie Burt)	Yes	No	No	No
*Rankin, Miss Mary D. (m. Miles Bronson)	Yes	Yes	?	?
Raymond, Merrill A.	No	Yes	Yes	?
Raymond, Mrs. M. A. (Agnes Lorish—Now Mrs. Raney)	Yes	Yes	Yes	Yes
*Rix, Miss Mabel (m. H. C. Long)	Yes	Yes	Yes	Yes
Robison, Benj. E.	No	Yes	Yes	Yes
Robison, Mrs. B. E. (Caroline Balch)	Yes	Yes	Yes	?
Rockwood, Bernard J.	No	No	No	Yes
Rowland, Leon E.	No	No	No	Yes
Rowland, Mrs. L. E. (Gladys Martin)	No	No	Yes	Yes
Scott, Job Hart	Yes	No	No	Yes
Scott, Mrs. J. H. (Carrie Vaughn)	Yes	No	No	?
*Scott, Miss Mildred A., M. D. (m. Newton H. Carman)	No	No	No	Yes
*Slaght, Miss Carrie E., M. D.	No	No	No	Yes
Smith, Mrs. Charles E. (Viola Ziegler)	No	Yes	Yes	Yes
Stannard, Mrs. Raymond E. (Marjorie Smith)	Yes	No	No	No
*Stever, Miss Edna M.	Yes	No	Yes	Yes
*Sweet, Miss Anna M. (m. Charles D. King)	Yes	Yes	Yes	?
Taft, George W.	Yes	Yes	Yes	Yes
Taft, Mrs. George W. (Mary Boyden)	?	Yes	?	?
Thomas, Mrs. R. C. (Winifred Cheney)	Yes	Yes	Yes	Yes
Thompkins, Charles E., M. D.	No	Yes	Yes	Yes
Thompkins, Mrs. Charles E. (May Bisbee)	Yes	Yes		Yes
*Watson, Miss Helen E. (m. Royal B. Hancock)	No	Yes	Yes	No
Weeks, Adoniram Judson	Yes	Yes	Yes	Yes
Weeks, Mrs. A. J. (Louise Scrimger)	Yes	Yes	No	Yes
Westcott, George W., M. D.	Yes	Yes	Yes	Yes
Westcott, Mrs. G. W. (Ellen Peckham)	No	Yes	No	No
Wilcox, Floyd C.	Yes	Yes	Yes	Yes
Wilcox, Mrs. F. C. (Emily Carder)	Yes	Yes	Yes	Yes

NOTE. Mrs. Lewis E. Martin (Nellora Clough) is a daughter of Dr. John E. Clough. John Clough Martin, Muriel Martin (Mrs. D. O. Smith) and Mrs. L. E. Rowland (Gladys Martin) are her children and the grandchildren of Doctor Clough.

Appendix

HOME MISSIONARIES

Home missionaries (including those now active) who were born or educated in Michigan: [1]

C. D. Allen, F. I. Blanchard, Rhena Brokaw, Marguerite Calder, Bertha Cheney, Bertha Clement, Ethelyn Cole, W. F. Cole, Harriet Cooper, Katherine Crawford, Thelma Cushing, Marian Davis, Frieda Dressel, Hazel Illsley, Abigail Johnson, Celia Kose, Alma Kurtz, Florence Latter, Jean Lund, Charles McHarness, Margaret McIntyre, Mildred McTyre, Eunice Monroe, Mary Murray, Corrine Potts, Frances Priest, B. E. Robison, Helen Tenhaven, Harry H. Treat.

In addition to the above the following persons, while neither born nor educated in Michigan, have served in the State as missionaries:

Mattie Anderson, Frances E. Broome, Edna Clingan, Bertha Kirschke, Hilda Krause, Mary Kwasigroch and Zelda Waters.

MISSIONARY ADMINISTRATORS

Among the special workers who have gone out from Michigan into service of wide Christian influence have been Dr. H. L. Morehouse, who served during several decades The American Baptist Home Mission Society as corresponding secretary; Dr. Lemuel C. Barnes, the secretary of English-speaking and Indian work of the same society and one of the originators of the Montana plan of interdenominational cooperative work in home mission territory; Mary Clark Barnes (Mrs. Lemuel Call Barnes), founder of The Neighbors League of America for work among non-English-speaking residents of America; also organizer of School of Americanization at Chautauqua Assembly, New York; Dr. John E. Smith, executive secretary of the New York Baptist State Convention (formerly of Michigan in same capacity); Dr. Rivington D. Lord, pastor of First Baptist Church of

---

[1] The list is incomplete. See first paragraph of Chapter Eleven.

Appendix

Williamsburg, Brooklyn, New York, and president of The American Baptist Home Mission Society; Hon. Grant M. Hudson, formerly a member of Congress, executive secretary of the Michigan Baptist State Convention and superintendent of the Michigan Anti-Saloon League; Mrs. Helen Crissman Thompson, first national field secretary of the World Wide Guild; Dr. James B. Fox, executive secretary of the Los Angeles Baptist City Mission Society; Dr. Carlos M. Dinsmore, secretary of Edifice Funds of The American Baptist Home Mission Society (formerly executive secretary of the Indiana Baptist State Convention); Dr. A. H. Bailey, formerly executive secretary of the East Washington and Northern Idaho Baptist State Convention. Dr. Harry S. Myers, secretary of the Department of Visualization of the Northern Baptist Convention; Dr. Henry T. McDonald, president of Storer College, Harpers Ferry, West Virginia; Elizabeth M. McDonald (Mrs. Henry T. McDonald), professor of French and German in Storer College; Rev. Archibald A. Forshee, executive secretary of the Boston Bethel City Mission Society; Dr. Henry M. Ford, formerly general secretary of Free Baptists; Dr. A. M. Bailey, pastor of the First Baptist Church of Lowell, Mass., and member of the Board of Managers of The American Baptist Home Mission Society; Dr. Mark Sanborn and Dr. John W. Hoag, ex-presidents of the B. Y. P. U. A.; John Scott, one time president of Bacone College, Oklahoma; Miss Elsie Kappen, field representative of the Council on Finance and Promotion of the Northern Baptist Convention; N. T. Hafer and Joseph W. Priest, Baptist benevolent institutions in Illinois; Dr. Reuben E. Manning, a former superintendent of Baptist City Missions in Chicago. Teachers in Negro schools: J. M. Arter, Sarah A. Benedict, Etta L. Hill, C. H. Lawrence, J. M. Manning, D. D. Martin, John M. Meighan, A. A. Myers, Mr. and Mrs. J. C. Newcomer, Mrs. Claire S. Newcomer, Elizabeth Sims, Bernard Terrell, Joseph M. Weaver.

ADDENDA

After the tabulation of foreign missionaries on pages 166-168 the additional data below was received by the writer through the kindness of Dr. Rivington D. Lord of Brooklyn and Miss Jessie K. Bates of the American Baptist Foreign Mission Society:

Of the children of the pioneer Free Baptist missionaries to India, Jeremiah and Hannah C. Phillips, Julia (Mrs. T. W. Burkholder), Harriet, Emily (Mrs. Albert J. Marshall), Nellie and Ida, educated in Michigan, were missionaries in India. Other Free Baptist foreign missionaries from Michigan: F. W. Brown, T. W. Burkholder, Milo J. Coldren, Mrs. (M. J.) Emma Smith Coldren, Z. F. Griffin, Robert D. Frost, Richard M. Lawrence, Albert J. Marshall, Melville C. Miner, Henry Colvil, Shirley H. Smith, M. D.

THE LAST WORD

As this volume is about to go to press, the writer (it may be more appropriate to say the *compiler*) desires to pay personal tribute to the Baptist men and women, living and dead, who have gone out from Michigan homes, churches and schools to add to the happiness and well-being of humanity, either as lay workers or as ministers of the gospel, *whose names have not been recorded herein.*

C. H.

MARCH 2, 1936.

INDEX

Index

Index

Index

Index

Lester, William, 25.
Limbocker, H. S., 89f.
Litchfield, Conn., 14.
Livingstone, David, 18.
Lockport, N. Y., 27.
Loomis, Harvey, 3.
Lord, Rivington D., 171.
Louisville, Ky., 55.
Lykins, Mr., 50.
Lyon, Albert J., 140.
Lyons, 84, 150.

Mack, Colonel Stephen, 21.
Mackinaw, 41.
Magill, D. T., 71.
Maine, 1, 118.
Maine Baptist Convention, 72.
Manro, Squire, 56-58.
March, John P., 38.
Marshall, 62, 78.
Marshall, Albert J., 171.
Marshall, Emily (Mrs. A. J.), 171.
Martin, Asa, 104.
Massachusetts, 1, 2, 5-7.
Massachusetts, Baptist Missionary Society of, 71, 75, 76, 110f.
Massachusetts Baptists, 17.
Mauck, J. W., viii.
Mauck, Willfred, viii.
May Anniversaries, 117f.
McCoy, Christiana (Heroine of the Michigan Wilderness), 47-55.
McCoy, Isaac, 27, 31, 37, 47-55, 75.
McIntyre, Mrs. Della Reynolds, viii.
Medical Missions, 144-147, 150-155.
Merrifield, Fred, 119.
Merrill, D., 71.
Merrill, D. D., 81.
Merrill, G. E., 71, 82.
Merrill, Moses, 73.
Merrill, T. W., 38, 63, 70-82.
Mexicans, 160.
Meyers, Harry S., 94f.
Miami Indians, 31, 36.
Michigan (Detroit) Baptist Association, 98f., 114f.

Michigan Baptist State Convention, viii, 19, 101-123.
Michigan Baptist Sunday School Association, 103.
Michigan Central College (Hillsdale), 83f.
Michigan Yearly Meeting, 91.
Mills, 3, 11.
Miner, Melville C., 171.
Minneapolis, 141.
Minnesota, 46, 137.
Missionary Administrators from Michigan, Appendix.
Missionary Convention (Baptist) of the State of N. Y., 27, 28, 56, 57, 58, 110f.
Missionary Review of the World, viii, 150.
Missionary Training School, 127.
Missions (magazine), viii, 70.
Mississippi, 16, 46.
Mississippi Valley, 17, 160.
Missouri, 14, 17, 161.
Monroe, Eunice, 127.
Montana, 46.
Mount Clemens, 22.
Mount Vernon, 131.
Murdock, J. N., 144-146.
Muskogee, Okla., 138.

Navajo Indians, 46.
Nealy, B. F., 91.
Negroes, 37, 51, 115, 138.
Nelson, John, 4.
Neri, 90.
Newell, Samuel, 5, 8, 11.
New England, 1, 2, 21, 28.
New Hampshire, 72.
New London, Conn., 28, 29.
New Mexico, 46.
Newton Theological Institution, 71.
New York, 1, 12, 17, 21, 57, 61, 72.
New York Baptist State Convention, 26, 58, 98. (See Missionary Convention of the State of New York.)

Index

Index

Rock Spring, Ill., 17.
Rock Spring Theological and High School, 18.
Roger Williams Guild, 118f.
Rogers, Ernest E., viii.
Romeo, 22.
Royal Ambassadors, 119, 120, 132.

Saginaw Valley Association, 130.
St. Clair River, 42.
St. John, 149.
St. Louis, 14, 15, 16.
St. Mark's College, 103.
St. Paul, 81.
Salem, Mass. (Tabernacle Congregational Church), 8.
Saline, 90.
Sandusky Bay, 42.
Saranac Lake, 151.
Sault Sainte Marie, 38, 39, 41, 43, 45, 58.
Savage, H. H., vii.
Schoolcraft, Henry, Esq. (U. S. Indian Agent), 39, 43.
Scott, Abigail Hart, 137-139.
Scott, Albert L., vii.
Scott, Dr. Anna K., 147.
Scott, Arthur P., 139.
Scott, George, 137-139.
Scott, George K., 139.
Scott, Prof. Harold, 142.
Scott, Job H., 142f.
Scott, John, 137-139.
Scott, Lida, 139-142.
Scott, Zar D., 139.
Sedgwick, Me., 71.
Selden, Colonel, 28.
Seneca Indians, 38.
Seymour, R. G., 107.
Sharp, D., 71, 75.
Shaw University, 138.
Shurtleff College, 18.
Sibley, Judge Solomon, 21, 23.
Sinex, President, 104.
Sioux Indians, 46.
Slaten, A. Wakefield, 119.
Slater, Leonard, 35, 37, 38, 58, 78.
Slater Station, 37.

Slavery, Negro, 105f.
Slaves, fugitive, 73.
Slayton, Helen E., viii, 97.
Sloan's Meadow, 3.
Smedner, William, 66.
Smith, A. W., 71.
Smith, John E., viii, 103.
Smith, Shirley H., 171.
Smith, William, 93.
South Carolina, 1.
South Dakota, 46.
Southern Baptist Convention, 117, 119.
Spanish, 15.
Spanish-American War, 159.
Spring Arbor, 83f.
Starr, Ruel, 61.
State Missions, 67, 69.
Staughton, William, 13.
Stephenson, E. M., 107.
Stewardship, 56-65, 156, 159.
Stone, A. B., 104f.
Stony Creek, 99.
Sudan, 154.
Swain, Anna Canada (Mrs. Leslie E.), viii, 48.
Swan, Dr. Ziba, 26.
Swatow, 140, 146, 147.
Swedes, 121.
Sweet, Anna, 123.
Swegles, Mrs. Harriet, 123.

Tappan, President (University of Michigan), 104.
Taylor, Lemuel, 99.
Temperance, 37, 61.
Tennents, the, 2.
Thomas Indian Mission Station (now Grand Rapids), 36, 37, 75.
Thompson, Mrs. Helen Crissman, 130-135.
Thompson, L. J., 91.
Thornton, Mr., 21.
Titterington, Mrs. Sophia B., 123.
Todd, Joseph, 25.
Todd, Major J. J., 21.
Tonawanda, 41.
Tonawanda Reservation, 38.

[179]

Index

COE HAYNE, a native of Michigan, was educated at Kalamazoo College (A. B., 1899) and at the University of Chicago (A. B., 1900; graduate work, 1900-1903). The honorary degree of Doctor of Letters was conferred upon him by Kalamazoo College in 1932. Ordained in 1907, he served in the pastorate at Eaton Rapids, Michigan (1907-1909), and in the Burlington Baptist Church, Salt Lake City, Utah (1916-1918). He was Y. M. C. A. interdivisional games manager in the Le Mans Area, France, 1918-1919. Since 1919 he has been connected with The American Baptist Home Mission Society as Recording Secretary, and as Secretary of Publicity, Literature and Research. Doctor Hayne has written extensively as a contributor to religious publications, and is also the author of *Old Trails and New*, *By-Paths to Forgotten Folks*, *Race Grit*, *For a New America*, *Young People and the World's Work*, *The God of Yoto*, *Red Men on the Bighorn*, *Vanguard of the Caravans*, *They Came Seeking*, and was a collaborator in the preparation of *America Tomorrow*, *The Road to Brotherhood* and *The Moccasin Trail*.